Iva Troj is an internationally acclaimed contemporary artist born in Plovdiv, Bulgaria. She studied art and design in the US and Scandinavia before establishing an art practice in the United Kingdom in 2012.
"Hello Troj" is based on her experiences growing up as a young protege during the last decade of Communism in Eastern Europe.
Iva Troj is a PhD and has exhibited both nationally and internationally. Her work is in private and museum collections in the UK, France, Ireland, Sweden, Norway, Germany, China, United States, South Africa, South Korea and Japan.

This book is for my late brother Troj whose presence in my life gifted me with just the right amount of magical thinking to fuel the rise above mediocrity my favorite author Kazuo Ishiguro so passionately writes about. Whatever foolish mess I got myself into, it was my late brother who kept me sane and gave my identity purpose. Communism, Cold War, poverty, walls, glass ceilings, misogyny, really poor taste in men, crossing borders that should not be crossed and burning bridges underneath my very feet, it all became manageable because Grief somehow made the seemingly impossible unavoidable.

Iva Troj

HELLO TROJ

You Can Leave Now

AUSTIN MACAULEY PUBLISHERS™

LONDON • CAMBRIDGE • NEW YORK • SHARJAH

A CIP catalogue record for this title is available from the British Library.

ISBN 9781398472815 (Paperback)
ISBN 9781398472822 (ePub e-book)

www.austinmacauley.com

First Published 2022
Austin Macauley Publishers Ltd®
1 Canada Square
Canary Wharf
London
E14 5AA

I would also like to extend my deepest gratitude to the people that came before me. They are the unsung heroes in my family who built homes and ploughed the earth, who fought the wars of others because they believed in a just future, who dug holes in the ground to hide partisans and Jewish refugees. Like my grandfather Troj who saved the lives of hundreds, was caught and tortured by the fascists more than once but continued fighting until Hitler was beaten and the war won. Like my grandmother Kerana who shaped me more than I can possibly know. This voice in my head that makes me uniquely me is as much hers as it is mine. This book is for all of them. I'm regifting their fates to the world because the world needs it.

1

Some stories are like tinnitus, they ring, buzz, hum, grind, hiss, and whistle in one's ear. One might think that telling them would make them go away, but no, they somehow manage to get louder and more persistent with time. Troj's story is like tinnitus with a loud choir on the side, like a Brecht play, choral interventions and all. Sometimes there are two stories colliding. One story circles around the circumstances surrounding Troj's death. The other story is the tinnitus that never goes away because it doesn't make any sense to anyone else but me.

My earliest memories of Troj come in bursts, with minutes, hours or days missing in-between.

I must be about six years old. I am sitting breathless and the street below me is blurred. I can smell my father's shaving cream in the drops of sweat on his back where my cheek is resting. My dad's back is rock-hard and difficult to cling to. I feel the memory of sharp pain in my ribs as Troj's fingers are sinking deeper and deeper into my waist. The color of my father's motorcycle is…I want to say blue, but that would be too matchy with the light-blue shirt and even lighter blue summer shoes. Bulgarian fathers didn't color coordinate in the '70s, it was against all rules of masculinity. The street noises are loud and the swishing sound of the wind makes them almost unbearable. Troj is hurting my ribs to a point where I have only two options: scream and get smacked or keep quiet and accept pain forever and ever, every day of the rest of my sweaty loud life. I scream.

Minutes missing.

Troj has red ears.

Minutes missing.

My father looks like a movie star with the sun shining behind him. He picks me up and carefully places me on the sidewalk beside the school fence. Troj is left behind at a nearby kindergarten amongst women in white coats and the occasional smelly cat with no name. I think of that all the way across the vast paved schoolyard. I fear for him before I enter the classroom and forget about him the second I see my friend Dina.

Hours missing. Motorcycle again. It is definitely light-blue. We are picking up Troj soon, but for a brief moment, I'm free to lift my head, look around and feel the wind in my hair. I see white coats and I smile wide. Who cares about the pain in my ribs? Troj is here.

To those of you who immediately thought that I was the sister of a mentally challenged child kept in an institution, I say: You should know better! Communist countries in the '70s were all about uniforms. Every profession had a uniform assigned to it and for the sake of effectiveness and expectations management, most uniforms were derivative of the lab coat. My school uniform was a dark-blue version of the lab coat and my only way to 'express' myself was a white detachable collar. Some kids had white embroidered collars (colorful things like flowers would have been unthinkable) and others had little pearl buttons. I expressed myself by not washing the dumb thing and letting it go grey.

Second memory.

We are in the gigantic corridor that separates the one-bedroom flats where almost everyone we know lives. Troj is watching a funny-looking small kid with big ears and his shiny new blue mini car. He is obviously envious of the kid, but there isn't much he can do, except hope for a turn in the car just for the sake of temporary friendship. Troj is a couple of years older and very much aware that his cuteness is starting to wear off so he makes himself as visible as he can. I understand his dilemma. He knows that he is a 'batko'–a Bulgarian word that means 'big brother'. 'Batko' is similar to the word 'kaka', which in Bulgarian means 'big sister' and is used to manipulate children into accepting a forever growing responsibility for slightly younger children so that adults don't have to. In this particular case, a 'batko' worth his title should not karate-kick little funny-looking boys out of their shiny new cars no matter how much they want to.

I am even older than Troj so I walk away and resume harassing my parents with my chatterbox ways.

Hours missing.

Later that night, as we get ready for bed, Troj folds his pocket knife and puts it in his pyjama pocket. Yes, our pyjamas had pockets. When you wear a dark-blue lab coat with a stupid collar all day, pyjamas trousers become a symbol of free thought. The pocket knife makes me anxious until Troj winks at me. We giggle for a while thinking 'sweet shenanigans' and start making our bed.

Our bed is not really a bed but a very hard kitchen sofa that can barely fit an averagely large drunken man. We have seen many a drunken man toss and turn on our sofa. It makes us happy to think that our bed somehow 'rejects' all the other people that try sleeping in it. We talk about it often.

Days missing.

Our mother has left us breakfast on the table and we wake up to the smell of chicken soup and pancakes. The kitchen sofa that we sleep in has a plywood back with a cherry-colored top. Underneath the top, I can see that Troj has used his pocket knife to carve the word 'granmass', which I assume is a new nickname for one of our grandmothers, our father's mother Ivanka. Ivanka is not a large woman so it's probably not about her 'grand mass'. I focus on the 'ass' aspect of the new word and start giggling. Troj is looking very pleased.

We both know that our mother is working this weekend. Our mother knows that we know. Nevertheless, she leaves a small note stating her working hours and explaining that there is chicken soup on the table and pancakes in the oven. Our sofa is about twenty centimetres away from the table so we can both see and smell the food. We read the note, fold it carefully and leave it on the washing machine just in case we need it later.

Hours missing.

Although I want to tell this story, death makes certain parts quite painful. Thinking about the mere frequency of vicious physical combat occurring on home alone days is making my stomach turn. It's like listening to a sermon about the suffering of Jesus and clearly remembering nailing his feet to the cross. Every time somebody utters the words 'all siblings fight', I think to myself, 'yeah, but yours didn't die'. The only thing that keeps me from wallowing in despair is remembering some kind of weird enjoyment in the kicking and screaming. I saw my little brother as an extension of my body and if I wanted to hurt myself, who was to stop me. Fighting provided much-needed relief in times when nobody listened to us or cared about our feelings. I can never be sure, but I think that Troj felt the same way. After threatening and hitting each other for a while, we would call it quits and go on with our usual business like nothing had happened. In any case, I don't remember any pain and I have no bruises from those fights. None that Troj caused anyway.

Our grandmother Ivanka was impatient and sometimes completely clueless when it came to caring for a child. Well, at least when it came to caring for the two of us. But I knew that she wasn't a bad person. She did some questionable things, but as much as I could tell, her intentions were never bad. She appeared quite determined in her ignorance, although she often argued with herself just

11

before she did something offensive towards us. That was a clear sign that she was somewhat aware of her shortcomings and cared for us in her own way. She just didn't know what to do with us, most of the time.

I couldn't stay mad at her for long. One: I was named after her and that was supposed to be a massive honour – she was a war hero after all, and two: she somehow always managed to show love while she was parenting us in all sorts of questionable ways. She would knit things for us and sometimes she would tell us stories. Once she wrapped herself around me to warm me up and held me until I stopped complaining about the cold.

Troj was not like me, he could really hold a grudge. Whenever Grandma Ivanka punished us for something that was obviously too much fun to be off-limits, I would laugh it off and forget about it. Troj, on the other hand, would withdraw in a corner and resent everyone for at least an hour or so.

In a way, all the bad things that we were punished for were things that shouldn't be off-limits for kids to do. Like swimming in the corn.

Another memory…

Sun is not scorching hot yet so it must be around 8 am. I wake up from the strong smell of fresh coffee and something buttery and lemony. Cake! There is a strange thunder-like sound and I wonder what, in the name of Lenin, is going on. I glue my face to the old window and I see a mountain of corn covering the entire front yard. The front door is open and I can see the back of a large dusty truck pulling out of our driveway. There is nowhere to walk – just a giant sea of corn with a mountain in the middle. I run out naked as I can't possibly waste any time dressing myself. As I open the door, I hear our grandmother shouting: "Go to the side around the stairs if you value your life, you vicious child! Corn is food and no filthy feet shall ever touch it. Do you freaking hear me?"

I ignore her while taking in the view. After ten seconds or so, she is shouting again. By that time, I am in love with the corn and no Ivanka can keep me away.

"You horrible little pig! I can hear you on the top of the stairs being vicious!"

My thoughts flatline until one emerges loud and clear: *I can swim*. My body floats by itself as I run on top of the corn. It's not that dangerous really, the piles around the corn mountain in the middle cover just about two-thirds of my body, but I am so fast that I can run without sinking. I do that for a second or two until I sink in a blessed sea of amazing softness. There is nothing like the feeling of being swallowed by smooth corn with my little smiling face floating just so that my mouth can take in air. My nose is already full of corn dust, but who cares as long as I'm alive enough to sense it all. Then I get dragged out of my dreamy state and the only thing I can see is a pair of big old wrinkled feet that haven't been washed since Ivanka fed the pigs this morning.

"But…but…please…noooooooooo!"

Heavy breathing.

Troj is already climbing on top of me in the corn as our grandmother is dragging me out leaving a trail in the corn sea.

"Troj…for dog's sake, run to the other side! Nooooooo! Troj, the mountain is too deep. Don't be stupid! Shhhh…calm…I'm calm, grandma…chill your beans." Smack.

Troj is screaming happily while swimming in the corn. The old woman just wouldn't give up. We wrestle for about two minutes until the corn is everywhere in scattered piles and Grandma Ivanka is exhausted to the point of heart failure. It's time for me to declare defeat and inspect my bruises.

There were bruises but no broken limbs. To this day, I have never broken any. I have some cuts here and there, but even they have healed quite nicely. My head has experienced some heavy hitting, though. So far, it hasn't led to anything worse than a bad headache.

After a battle like that, I would run to my older cousin next door and get patched up. She wouldn't have disinfectants and bandages – just some old band-aids and her father's eau de cologne, which kind of served the same purpose. My older cousin was so beautiful and clever that I would forget all about Grandma Ivanka and indulge in following my cousin around their vast garden asking her questions about life and the universe while trying to ignore my bleeding, aching and heavily perfumed knees. After a couple of hours, I would return home with a huge cucumber and some strawberries to give to Grandma, but Ivanka wouldn't deserve any strawberries so she would get a half-eaten cucumber at most.

By the time Grandma went numb from yelling, Troj would have disappeared. That was what he did. Sometimes I would find him stroking a donkey's or a horse's forehead in the middle of the pumpkin field. It would be quite unclear how the donkey or horse ended up in the middle of the pumpkin field. Did Troj find it there because that's where it always was? Or did Troj lead it there just so they could be alone? It was a clever move either way. It would take Ivanka ages to reach him there. Also, it would be quite funny to watch her trying to run around the pumpkins with her floppy tits jumping up and down while birds are eating her brain. Sorry…got carried away.

Sometimes I'd find Troj talking to some old Romani man on the other side of the village. I would never dare tell Grandma about that. Romani people were another off-limits thing on the list, especially the old scary ones with no teeth.

This one time, I couldn't find him at all, so I had to wait for him by the neighbour's house, just out of Ivanka's visual range and well positioned so I could see the street and the entrance to the house at the same time. It was almost completely dark when Troj finally showed up. He was so tired that he almost fell asleep in my arms while walking the last hundred yards to the house. We were met by our grandfather who was genuinely worried. Grandpa Troj was not a very tolerant man. But worrying about the boy somehow made him mellow. Seeing him and not Ivanka waiting by the entrance was a relief. I had no energy for her that day.

Troj wouldn't talk about his feelings much, but I knew he hated being punished for stupid things. As said, he didn't forgive and forget easily. I was probably the only one, in addition to our mother, whose sins and transgressions were forgiven. No one knows why. After all, I was the one that always initiated the bad things. Everyone knew that, but they punished both of us anyway. It wasn't fair, I thought, so I tried to make sure he enjoyed himself as much as he possibly could before we could be stopped. That's probably why he forgave me. I'm just guessing though.

Grandma Ivanka reminded me of this children's book character that fired up my imagination more than any other. I can't, for the life of me, remember the exact name of the book except it was something something 'Pencil-Nose', which was what the name of the character would be if it was accurately translated from Russian to Bulgarian and then to English. This 'Pencil-Nose' was a boy with a pencil for a nose. Other than that, he was just an ordinary boy until one day he discovered that he could draw really well and whatever he drew came to life. Just the mere thought of that happening made my heart beat faster. The most interesting part of the book was the chapter when 'Pencil-Nose' fell sick with a really high fever and started drawing horrible evil people that came to life. The thought of that happening made my heart beat so fast I'd almost faint. 'Pencil-Nose' was sleep-drawing and didn't know what he was doing, so he was still a lovely character, after all. In my mind, our grandmother Ivanka was 'Pencil-Nose' who was sleep-drawing one feverish night and out of the wall came our Aunt Eunice.

Another memory: Dad and Troj are attaching a small motor to Troj's handmade skateboard. We are outside the two-storey building where some of the poor employees of the Plovdiv Agricultural Institute live with their families. It is very clear where the line between poor and not-poor lies. The poor seem to mostly work with their hands and wear two-piece uniforms in blue. The not-poor wear normal clothes or white lab coats. Some of them wear a tie. My father loves a good tie so that's a pity, I guess. The not-poor live mostly in the centre of my hometown Plovdiv. Some of them live in villas.

Troj is trembling with anticipation. He knows that whatever Dad touches turns into a mechanised toy with unexpected fun features. Our father's hands are rough but soft to the touch. I have no idea how that works, but I'm telling it exactly as I remember it.

I am carefully watching a drop of strawberry jam on Troj's face that looks like it is just seconds from landing on Dad's face. I am also carefully watching Dad's quick fingers. I don't really know what he is doing exactly, or how he is doing it, but that doesn't stop me from being absolutely one hundred percent sure that we will be in toy-robot heaven soon.

We are not alone. At least twenty children live in our house and most of them are outside watching our father operate tiny screwdrivers and gadgets that look like little turbines. Some of the kids are excited, but the majority of them, especially the boys, are envious. The device looks like something that would take one fat boy and a wrong turn in the nearby ditch to break to pieces. The thought on everyone's mind right now is: *Please, let me be the one to break this!*

What can I say? Our dad likes delicate beautiful machines. It is quite tragic that he was put in charge of the monster that is the Agricultural Institute refrigeration system. In a way, both our parents' work involved managing monsters. Our mother operated something she called 'The Elephant' at the Oncology Department of First State Hospital in Plovdiv. It was Russian, born in the late '50s, filled a whole room and somehow either cured or killed people with cancer. Some of those people were children, but I didn't want to think about them, so I focussed on the old wrinkled people with no teeth on Grandma Ivanka's off-limits list.

Troj can't wait any longer. He is fidgeting worse than I do when faced with a swim-in-corn-or-wrestle-Ivanka dilemma. Even Dad is getting impatient. Either that or he knows that his fun is over as soon as he is done wiring because that one fat kid will get on the board eventually and drive into the nearby ditch.

Minutes missing.

Troj looks like a small-size superhero flying around on the skateboard. His hair is really long and the side pockets of his shorts are flapping noisily. The soundtrack of this memory is 'Splendor' by M83, although M83 were not even born yet.

Fourth or fifth memory, not sure…Ivanka is screaming at me while she tries to put clothes on my skinny little body. She barely manages to pull a semi-clean tank-top over my head when I wriggle myself free. I run away with just the top on, off to the grass-covered field behind the house. She knows where I am headed and tries to intercept. She fails and begins hollering incoherently: "Dare to just…no panties…the neighbours will see you. You silly goose…cane…will paint you stripy…when I catch you."

I have run too far so I can only hear an echo. I turn to double check. There she is, half of her body is under the grass and her walking stick is pointing at me in the same way Stalin does in Grandfather's pictures. The grass is now almost up to my shoulders, and it becomes difficult to run. She comes closer. The wart, the wicked one, with the hair in the middle that looks like a bird's head, has changed color.

I can hear Troj's laughter, and I get somewhat annoyed because I'm just about to meet the stick. Ivanka is so funny-looking though.

The thing is that Aunt Eunice is about to visit. That is why having clothes on is so important. The woman is the kind of vicious creature that only exists in fairy tales. Though this one is for real. She cuts my nails so deep that blood starts dripping. Then she forces me to sit with my hands in soap and water for several hours to 'loosen the dirt'.

"Dirrrty pig are ya," she says, looking triumphantly at me. I try to forget the misery and disappear in our black and white television that now shows Bulgaria's premier gymnastics star spinning and turning in completely implausible pirouettes and leaps.

"I am Maria Gigova," I shout fondly and repeat the girl's tricks in my head.

"Ya ain't, ya' little toad," sputters Aunt, and I'm off to the grass again, soap dripping from my spongy trembling hands and a head full of evil plans of revenge.

Troj is already in the middle of the field giggling his little head off.

2

'Pencil-Nose' did exactly what her daughter told her to do. Eunice made life unbearable for everyone but the two of them, or so it seemed. Apparently, Ivanka hated Eunice's ways just as much as the rest of us did. She confessed to our mother on her deathbed. Then she smiled wide, tears filled her eyes and she said that she was sorry. Good for you, 'Pencil-Nose'!

Eunice has a daughter and her name is Mimmi. I used to love playing with cousin Mimmi, but the unmistakable hierarchy had us separated in different categories. Mimmi was for some reason more valuable than Troj and I put together. There was no reason for it other than the fact that Mimmi was Eunice's daughter. Later on, I added two and two together and figured out that it wasn't about us kids at all. It was our mother who didn't fit in. Our mother is the sweetest and the most caring person that ever walked the earth, but that was of no importance to my father's family. It was all about her blood, or 'circus blood' as Grandma Kerana called it.

'Circus blood' is what makes plants and animals magical. It is also the fabric of premonition dreams and the little voice in your head that tells you to put your knees together when a man's eyes change color. Dogs have circus blood, and sometimes pigs do too. And off-limits Romani people with no teeth have it. Eunice had a different name for it – 'gypsies' she called us. I didn't really understand it. The so-called 'circus blood' was an abstract concept that I couldn't place anywhere on the map of things we learned in school or from family and friends. In my head, Troj and I were no different from other kids.

Truth is, I don't really know exactly where I came from, which may be the reason why I never truly felt at home anywhere. I was about nineteen or twenty years old when I first heard about our Macedonian Greek heritage. In Eunice's world that was more or less proof that we were of Romani origin. She put the gypsy label on us simply because we came from a place where everyone was mixed and nobody knew exactly where their ancestors came from. The whole Balkan peninsula is like a mouth that opens and closes to let people in and out of Europe. Macedonians and Bulgarians are not that different from each other. The things that separate us are mostly ideas that don't make much sense, like the fact that some Bulgarians still believe in 'Bulgaria on Three Seas' – an idea rooted in vaguely documented eleventh-century glory and powered by nationalism and ignorance. But carelessly giving away labels and adding fuel to nationalist fires was what our Aunt Eunice did best. At first, I thought that she was a special kind of stupid, the kind that didn't watch her tongue. As I grew older, I realised that she was dangerous and very much aware that her tongue could ruin a person's life or even kill them.

Our mother's mother, Grandma Kerana, on the other hand, was not the kind that tolerated offensive words. "Your words are painful," she would say in an angry voice. But whenever she was in the same room as our father's mother and sister, she would keep to herself no matter what they said. I found that odd because Grandma Kerana was otherwise very quick to defend anyone who was treated unfairly. She would break the silence occasionally only to suggest alternatives to our aunt's labels. That's how 'circus blood' came about – it came to replace the very offensive 'mangal' that Eunice threw at us every time we did anything she found to be 'cocky'. 'Mangal' is the Turkish word for a chafing dish or charcoal brazier, also the Bulgarian equivalent of 'nigger'.

The labels made very little sense to me because dark skin was something most Bulgarians had in common, especially in the summer when everyone was sunburned from crispy dark brown to almost black. Our father's side of the family went from Grandpa Troj, whose skin was very dark, the type of dark that made him invisible in black and white photos, to Ivanka, who was fairly light skinned. Troj and I were somewhere in the middle. On our mother's side of the family, skin color varied from light brown to pinkish white. Grandma Kerana's skin color varied because she was always out and about in her garden, but I remember her as being fairly light-skinned.

As said, none of this skin color business made any sense. It didn't really matter how Eunice chose her words, in one way or another, she always meant that I was a 'bad seed' and it couldn't be helped because it was 'in my blood'. I could almost see the word 'gypsy' next to my name on my birth certificate, although that would be impossible as I had a Bulgarian name and most Romani people had Turkish-sounding names.

It has been a while since Bulgaria was a communist country. History has been altered many times and a lot has changed in the way people perceive historical events. The Russian 'brotherhood' was all the rage when I was a child.

We called the Russians 'братя' (brothers) and 'товарищи' (comrades), but the similarities between our people were more or less entirely manufactured. We were more like the much hated Turks than we cared to admit.

When it comes to discussing their origin, Bulgarians always seemed confused to me. Even now, almost three decades since the Berlin wall went down, the mere reminder of our Mongolian origin would confuse some people. For them, 'Asian' is the same as the low-pay Vietnamese workers that once filled the shoe and canned food factories. There couldn't be any similarities there. Black people didn't exist in any of the literature with the exception of 'Uncle Tom' – a book that made us believe black people were extinct, much like the dodo. But nothing was more confusing than our relationship with Turkey. Five hundred years of bloodshed and Islamisation under Ottoman rule left Bulgaria torn to tiny scattered pieces and such a thing is never easy to forgive. The hatred that we felt towards our Turkish neighbours was mutual and nobody cared enough to conceal it. It was all out in the open. We were told stories about Turks and the Ottoman Empire and it all sounded like it was happening in the present. The stories became more and more gruesome as we grew older, and there were plenty of movies to make these stories seem even more real. As a child, I was particularly interested in stories about Islamisation. The stories varied somewhat between history teachers, but the basics were the same: 'Bands of Turkish soldiers would ride on horsebacks around the country forcing Bulgarian people to give up Christianity. If they didn't accept Islam as their true faith, their children would either be slaughtered or taken away.' At this point, I would raise my hand and ask: "Where were the children taken?" The teachers would answer that 'the girls were raped and the boys were forced to become soldiers'. As they tried to continue, I would interrupt them again: "What happened with the children after that?" Teachers would sigh and tell me that they 'all became Turks with Turkish names'. That answer was so far from satisfactory that I had to ask: "Did they move to Turkey then?" This was usually when I was told to sit down, shut up and let the rest of the class 'gain some knowledge'. At this point, every kid in the classroom, all fifty of them, was on board with the questions so they were all told to sit down and shut up. Everyone was unhappy, and it was all my fault. But what could I do? There were so many unanswered questions. For example, nobody knew what it meant to be raped. I asked around and, believe me, nobody knew. We had all seen rape scenes in movies about the Ottoman Empire, but they consisted of girls' clothes being torn off their bodies and that

19

was that. We knew a little more about being soldiers, but rape was a mystery just as much as sex was. Nobody was willing to explain these things to us.

One thing that always left me confused was the fact that no matter how many times I did my statistical equations, I ended up thinking that the people that were forced to accept Islam were the same people that Eunice called 'mangals'. This conclusion led me to the next big question: 'How come these people weren't pardoned when Bulgaria was freed from the Turks?' They never wished to become Turks, they were forced, I thought and wondered why most of them still lived isolated, poor and miserable lives. It wasn't because I cared. It was a purely selfish thing to worry about. If what Eunice said was true, and I was indeed a 'mangal', I could one day be sent to live with them. And even more troublesome was the thought that I would be there without Troj. The thing was, Eunice would have never had the guts to call my brother anything, especially 'mangal'. There were two reasons for that: One: because he was a boy, and two: because he was our grandfather's namesake. Grandpa Troj adored him and the feeling was mutual. It was a line never to be crossed as long as Grandpa lived. Our mother and I were definitely alone in this.

There was only one place where I felt at home – Grandma Kerana's house in the Sakar Mountains. Sakar borders both Greece and Turkey, and there was a distinct uniqueness about the Sakar villages. They were Bulgarian, Greek, Turkish, Macedonian and, at the same time, neither. It was like the Sakar people belonged there and nowhere else. Their villages were scattered around the mountain tops along the green, purple and poppy-red fields running almost vertically and coloring the mountains like a child's finger-painting.

Bad things happened to people who left the mountain for the cities below. When they left Sakar, they mixed with the rest of the population and there was nobody to cure them and heal them in the way that only a Sakar woman could. Nobody could describe how this healing was done, but women like our grandmother somehow knew. The only person that she couldn't cure and save was herself.

Grandma Kerana and Grandpa Troj died within months of each other in their respective parts of the country – one in Granit and one in the Sakar Mountain. Troj and I were left without protection roughly at the same time.

We didn't spend much time with Grandma Kerana. She had way too many grandchildren and some of them were not to my liking, mainly because they were boys and took away Troj from me on a regular basis. Besides, Sakar Mountain was too far from Plovdiv and Grandma Ivanka was only forty kilometres away.

There was something very significant that separated our mother's from our father's side of the family. Grandma Kerana didn't lie. She would keep very quiet about certain things, but if we asked, she would answer in short and exact sentences, without hesitation and without looking for childish words that we would easily understand. Even if telling the truth meant causing herself or somebody else pain, she would still tell it. She would tell it in a way that made the pain purposeful, like the pain somehow made the story whole. No pain, no story, simply put. We were told that lies spread poison in our brains and to this day I can't tell a lie, not even a tiny innocent one, without feeling nauseous.

I just wish that we had had the nerve to ask her all the questions that kept us awake at night.

I've always wanted to relive those short visits to the mountains, but I suppose some things can never happen again. There was something mysterious in that hot summer air and definitely something in the soil. The size of the vegetables and the flowers Grandma kerana grew in her garden were like something out of a fairy tale or a horror movie, depending on the mood of the day. She could take one single tomato and make a huge bowl of salad out of it and spices.

The life our mother's mother created for herself was definitely different than what was going on in our lives down below. She was no friend of routine other than what was required by nature itself. She shaped the world as she went along. Her house was like the walking house in Hayao Miyazaki's *Howl's Moving Castle*, furniture was always moving around and new things were created every day, either by her or by her partner Slavi. The smell of lavender, fresh wool and wet tea leaves filled every nook and cranny of the old house. The mats she wove embraced everything like the endless vertical fields that painted the mountains red, green and blue. The chestnut tree, featuring Grandpa Slavi underneath carving toys with his folding knife, marked the centre of the universe.

Grandpa Slavi was nobody's and everybody's grandfather. Our mother's father was another man, he was the face from the yellowing photos on Grandma's rose-scented linen closet – a boyish face with an old man's eyes. Troj had his eyes.

Our mother's father died when our mother was only seven. He was the sheriff at a time 'with no cars and motorbikes', I am guessing from the mid 1940s to 1950. He rode his horse around all the villages in his precinct and watched over his people, lending a helping hand whenever needed, solving a petty theft here and rescuing a cow stuck in the mud there. One winter day, he was on his way home when the immense mountain exploded in a blizzard. He found himself in the middle of a terrifying sea of snow. He wandered for days through the storm, the wind tore loose at his body, snow and ice filled his shoes and his horse was dying. When he finally found his way home to Grandma Kerana, it was too late for healing.

I am not proud of the way that I've kept these stories to myself. I used to tell them to my son but only occasionally to my daughter. I don't know why that is. Maybe I underestimate the people in my life assuming they would never truly understand, or maybe it's because I feel different from them. I eventually broke the silence about a decade ago when we attended a cousin's wedding – involuntarily, I should add. My mother really wanted us there, but I refused, mainly because my daughter Saga's Swedish father was traveling with us. Mother didn't give up, though. She somehow managed to talk Saga's father into going to the wedding so I agreed at the end and we drove the three hundred kilometres to a small town just below the Sakar Mountain. I told him as much as I could manage, but my stories only made him laugh, which was exactly the reaction I was expecting. The more he laughed, the scarier it got.

Right from the door, he was embraced and almost carried away by chatting women, every one of them ready to adopt him into her flock of sons. He was placed in the middle of the patio, the cousins ran after watermelons and booze and the food was served, as if by magic, in a minute. My mother's older sister, Dora, knew that Saga's father was a programmer so she started blaming 'Swede' for her non-functioning computer while my cousin's wife Mary fed him dried meat. "Do not worry about all the bullet bits. It is a wild boar that we have shot in the woods. Hubby bought a new car and it is much easier to hunt now. See here!" My second aunt took out a stack of pictures of herself dressed in camouflage, AK4 in one hand, a dead rabbit in the other. Her grey hair was cut really short and she smiled like a little girl as if the automatic weapon was a lollipop and the camouflage overall a princess' dress. She looked so damn happy in those hunting pictures.

'The Swede' was plastered in three minutes, something he received many compliments for. Holding one's drink is a virtue among men in my family, but they were quite understanding about 'the nature of the Swede'. After almost losing consciousness, he was sent on a mission. He was handed a giant knife and shoved into a basement. Meat must be cut for Aunt to do 'the frying'. There were dead animals hanging from the ceiling and he jumped up and down cutting little puny bits of meat. My aunts wouldn't stop laughing and pointing, but he was just too drunk to care. Then he was allowed to fire my cousin's gun, or perhaps it was my aunt's gun…Nobody remembers exactly. I'm rather happy nobody died that day.

The women on my mother's side of the family are all the same – storytellers, entrepreneurs, providers and mind readers, every single one. You can't hide anything from them. It took some time to understand it, but by the time I was four years old, I knew that it was pointless to try to con them or lie. "Oi you, the pen you're holding behind your back…Was it Gianni Rodari or H. C. Anderssen who got an extra princess somewhere among them ugly ducklings?" "You! Peter, the neighbour on the other side of the village, has got a pair of smelly socks in the letterbox, I think I know that you are to blame." There were two hundred children living in the neighbourhood, but she immediately knew that it was I who 'done it'.

Maybe circus blood was just the blood of mountain folks.

3

Memories are an odd thing, especially childhood memories. There is no obvious logic to the way I've stored them. They come back randomly, like short but intense dreams. In a flash, I'd be standing in the middle of Grandma Kerana's kitchen, her flowery dress wrapped around my little body and a poppy crown placed proudly on my head, spiralling curls holding it together. I'd be singing loudly, jumping up and down like a pig drunk on fermented cherries, until Grandma's voice echoed from the seed cellar below the patio: "Greatness travels quietly, little one." Her words would somehow make sense. I'd stop jumping and lower my voice, changing the tune to a song I'd heard on the radio. I'd follow her wishes like in a dance. The more I practised, the more complicated the movements became. Then, all of a sudden I'd be transported below the mountains into the dusty, barren city with all its noise and ugliness. The dance would stop and all the words would fall to the ground like shadows, their meaning breaking into million unrecognisable pieces.

Back in the city, far, far away from the Sakar Mountain, I would hold Troj near me, smelling his skin and trying to figure out where he'd been all morning, and I'd whisper in his ear: "Greatness travels quietly, little one."

"You are such an idiot," he would say and shove me to the floor.

"I will crush you with my body," I'd scream.

"Yeah, because you are so fat," he'd answer and run behind the bathroom door closing it with a bang. Hearing his laughter would enrage me and I'd spend a good fifteen minutes shouting and hitting the door with my tiny fists.

We never did this kind of thing at Grandma Kerana's house. Life there was slow, calm and didn't call for any kind of erratic behavior. Left alone, we would just sit quietly, read or play in the garden. But three hundred kilometres away, in our town home, all bets were off. The constant noise, the endless trail of patients that our mother saw outside work, all the drama and interference, made us crazy.

Needless to say, childhoods below the mountains were different, not better or worse, just numbingly different. Every time our parents dragged us out of the mountains and down below, I would spend weeks feeling like an alien offspring

24

much too rooted in my foreign ways. And it didn't help that my favourite friend, neighbourhood aristocrat named Vanja (her father was an engineer), would periodically look at me like I was covered with scales.

Vanja was a nervous character, and more often than not, my foreign ways made her jumpy. I so wanted to be her friend though, mostly due to the fact that her mother was in a wheelchair. That was a very rare thing. In those days, handicapped people were kept inside, and since I hadn't met any, I was curious to know about her life and especially the part about the wheelchair.

The gossip around the institute could be summarised as follows: "A beautiful but aggressive husband with boyish eyes, disobedient children, an empty grey city and a dream that never became reality had made her almost completely immobile. She was so worn out by life that she just collapsed one day. She had one stroke, a number of illnesses (with complicated names) after that and then another stroke."

Mom's take on that gossip added a parallel story about Vanja's mother doing 'what we all must vow to never do'. She had 'sold her body and mind to the religious nothing and freed herself from the responsibility of having a soul'.

Don't misunderstand me, our mother believes in all sorts of circus blood things, like 'the link that holds us all together' and having a sixth sense about things. She also believes in some kind of a god or gods and the power of lit candles, especially the power of lit candles. But she doesn't believe in making God responsible for one's own fate. Let's be clear about that.

Whenever I dropped by to pick Vanja up for Komsomol youth group meetings, drama class or sports, I would see her mother sitting in the wheelchair reading a meaningless magazine on dog breeds or just browsing through last week's paper. She didn't have a dog, but that simple fact didn't seem to matter much. I would often initiate a conversation on the topic of Jesus. I'm not sure if I was curious about her religious beliefs or just wanted to see what would happen if an actual religiously themed conversation took place. People were not exactly open about their faith back then as religion was strictly forbidden and talking about it could get one in some serious trouble. Still, we would talk for a while, and Vanja would pretend to enjoy the conversation while nervously pressing a Garfield the Cat cushion against her chest. We didn't have Garfield comics in Bulgaria, but somehow, somebody had come across a picture and copied it on to a cushion.

Typically, it would take about ten minutes before the dialogue degenerated. "Ah, that pesky science!" Once I told her about something heard on Radio Free Europe – a pirate radio channel that was sending real news and not communist propaganda. Dad had heard that National Geographic had published a story about Jesus being 'a black man with curly hair'. That enraged Vanja's mother and she started shouting, "Lies, horrible lies." One of her eyes teared up. "Jesus had long blond hair and was a virgin just like his mother Mary. End of story! Stop fidgeting and leave 'The Cat' alone!"

I have always thought that one needs a parallel reality to anchor the reality one is experiencing. I used Troj for that all the time. I would always check with him to see if my experiences made any sense. Whatever he told me, I would remember. But then that second reality would need a third to make it relevant so Troj would check with Mom and so on in an endless chain. I guess we all do that. That's how histories are made.

That chain was broken violently when communism ceased to be the ruling structure in Bulgarian society. Everything just lost its meaning and the stories changed. Some people never recovered from the mere shock of reality breaking into incomprehensible pieces.

About a decade before that happened, during my childhood years, communist ideology still ruled the land. It was like a fog just above everyone's head. One in ten or so thousand people would have the means to raise their head above the fog and look around, but the rest of us remained below, staring at an impenetrable foggy ceiling. From the day we were born, our destinies were given away to the rickety structure that held our society together and we had no say other than in the tiny details. In a way, it was comforting. Unless you were 'a cripple', mentally ill or had a Turkish sounding name, your fate was somewhat guaranteed, your survival somewhat secured and your future more or less defined. One way or another, we all ended up serving The Party and that worked just fine for most people. But mountain life differed and that was what I mostly liked about it, alongside our grandmother's cosy and yet mysterious house. The mountains seemed just outside the reach of The Party. There were no communist leaders to tell you what to do and what to believe in. Only endless vertical fields and a faraway view of Greece constantly reminding us that there was a world outside ours that we knew nothing about.

Up there, fate was freelancing.

I don't ever remember being picked up from the mountain house. The differences between Sakar and the city were so vast that every departure was a shock to the system. Maybe that was why our grandmother wouldn't travel anywhere except if it was a life and death thing that needed her attention. Traveling was for her 'a violent experience'. Traveling 'took you out of your ordinary world and forced you to trust strangers, lose sight of your home and be in a constant state of unbalance. You owned nothing but the essential things such as 'air, sleep, dreams, the mountains, the sea, the sky'. "But isn't that a good thing, owning the sky and all?" I would ask.

She would smile quietly and answer: "Well, beauty does the same thing. And that's enough for me."

My Sakar Mountain related chain of realities must have been broken more than once for me to remember nothing about the journeys back to the city. Maybe our parents had to drag us out of the mountain world kicking and screaming, forcing us back into the fog. Or maybe they took us while we were sleeping. In a way, we had to be re-educated before we reached Plovdiv. Not fitting in was dangerous in those days. Our mother did it in subtle ways, often against our father's wishes. She would fill the backseat of our tiny Russian car with children's books, most of them translated from Russian. She bought them and put them there. Before the tiny car existed, she would carry the books in her bottomless purse.

Most of the books were about communist heroes who all too often died in the end. Their death wasn't supposed to make us sad because they sacrificed themselves for the communist ideas and thus for 'the greater good'. They made us sad, though, until we started laughing at them.

The first episode of *Star Trek* I ever watched, many years later, was about the Klingon Empire. I couldn't stop laughing at the Klingons' willingness to die for an abstract notion of honour that was somehow rooted in violence. My American friends, all devoted trekkies, were appalled and shocked by my laughter, but I couldn't help myself – the Klingons reminded me of the heroes in those Russian books scattered around the backseat of our car.

In the city, everyone was more or less marching around keeping to a never-changing routine of early breakfasts, work, communist meetings, garlic-smelling dinners, lots of alcohol and sexless nights. Most evenings, adults would gather for some pre-dinner gossip, men on one side of an often struggling garden, women on the other.

The more I adapted to everyone else's city-bound rhythm, the more I forgot about the Sakar Mountain and Grandma. My willingness to forget, adapt, serve and please, annoyed the life out of Troj. He called me 'servile' and scratched my arm until it started bleeding.

4

Our parents drove to Grandma Ivanka's house almost every weekend. Sometimes they would leave us there for weeks. Unlike mountain people, our father's parents were not the patient kind. They didn't like the fact that we were 'undisciplined city kids' and somehow our 'blood' was always an issue. Aunt Eunice was the only one who called me 'mangal' to my face, but people gossiped and called us 'wild' and 'unruly'. This kind of attitude would often spread to the children we played with. All of a sudden, they would start hiding their toys and making up excuses not to go to the river or play with the horses with us. But some people seemed to like us, especially me. One or two villagers would tell me that I had 'the gift' – the gift to read people, that is. Maybe I got it from Grandma Kerana, they assumed. Or maybe it was 'the blood'. I would walk right up to people and tell them what they were thinking. It either spooked them or it made them smile.

That so-called 'gift' was something I learned out of necessity. The men in my childhood were so unpredictable that it was up to me to quickly figure out what their words and actions meant. The slightest arm movement could be followed by a kick, a slap, or something much worse. That same movement could also carry the promise of an embrace.

In a way, I had no choice but to accept the stupid gift. I could almost agree with Eunice that it was indeed a curse. Because, you see, I was taught to probe for needs. It was the work of women to read the faces and movements of men. It was a never-ending chore – probing and waiting, cataloguing events and reactions and matching them with corresponding needs, in neat columns in the mind. Every day. Every night.

I still do this. I probe and catalogue. But I probe for the needs of children, friends and pets. Men are almost never on my radar these days. Only occasionally, every ten years or so, I would meet somebody who is just like me – a skilled prober. The fact that I so willingly submit to the equally gifted has made me prone to life-altering mistakes. The problem is that people probe for different reasons. Some people look for things that they can take or use. Some people look for weaknesses. Some people look for desires that match their own. The key is to understand the quixotic nature of the need-fulfilling process. It is very egotistical at its best and it backfires all the time. It is like a work of art. You look at something or somebody through your own lenses then you interpret what you learn and turn it into something else. And when you are done with 'it', you renounce your ownership of 'it'. 'It' becomes somebody else's to do whatever he or she wishes to do. Once you fulfil a need, it is up to them. Some people would do the same for you. They are as exceptional as Troj was. Some people wouldn't even notice that you did something to ease their pain or make them smile. Or maybe you didn't make them smile because you misunderstood and it backfired. Everyone gets it wrong sometimes, Romanipen or gadjo. Some people would resent you for it or ask for more just because they are used to having their needs met. Some people wouldn't stop asking for more until you have nothing left. Some people wouldn't stop asking for more if it killed you.

I have met all kinds.

The irony of this entire 'circus blood' business was that it wasn't our mother whose blood was 'circus' in the way Eunice meant it, it was hers and our father's. I don't have all the facts, but according to Grandma Ivanka (seriously sloshed on Christmas Eve), my great grandfather Trifon, the man our father was named after, 'went all bonkers head over heels' over a Romani girl. He kidnapped her, because 'that's what you did to Romani girls back then', and married her. Years later, I put two and two together and understood that the young girl and the village blind storyteller were one and the same. The old woman had drowned herself in the well when I was very young, but I remember her vividly. It wasn't the muddy water in the well that suffocated her. It was something else. I remember her watching me with her blind eyes and sitting with her trembling henna-painted hands in her lap while the village women slashed her open with their evil tongues.

I've always thought of Romani women as insanely beautiful. Other little girls wanted to be princesses while I dreamed of becoming a Romani queen. I would trade pink dresses and glass slippers for long wavy hair and henna-painted hands any day. A Romani princess would be mystical, unpredictable, and most importantly, she would have amazing long hair, something I wasn't permitted to have.

One thing was certainly true – Romani women were by definition unpredictable.

Every day on my way to secondary school, I would pass the Romani houses. School started so early that busses were barely running and I had to take a shortcut through the outskirts of Plovdiv. Monday mornings were the most fun as the obligatory Sunday festivities were still going on. Every balcony was a miniature stage. Beautiful women in colorful clothes were still clapping hands and voicing their sorrows loudly as the morning embedded their every move in milky fog. I had the habit to stare, just as my daughter Saga now does when she studies things 'on the inside'.

One Monday morning, I saw the most beautiful living being I had ever seen. Her fiery red hair reached all the way down to her knees; her body was the body of a goddess; her arms and hands were covered with henna paint – the mysterious holy wordings of passion and desire. I stared at her for a while in a dreamlike state until I woke up in complete and utter shock. A stone as big as my fist hit the pavement just millimetres from my feet. Her naked red haired vagina stared back at me as her voice echoed through the fog: "Eat me with your eyes, you Bulgarian piece of shit."

As much as I want to tell my story with the touch of sarcasm that it deserves, the love I feel for the people in it, even Ivanka, stops me from celebrating the irony of it all. The feelings I have for Aunt Eunice are there by proxy as I adored my cousin Mimmi. But, weirdly enough, the person who I felt most connected to, apart from Troj, was his namesake.

Grandfather Troj was a difficult man to figure out…for everyone else. I can almost swear that I felt him in my head, which made Grandma Ivanka a little jealous. She didn't get him at all. And she complained. She complained about him when she was awake and when she slept. Mostly, she complained that he didn't eat her food. She would wave a big wooden spoon saying: "An idiot on TV said that the way to a man's heart is through his stomach. Cowshit. There's no freaking way." In reality, no one wanted her food; it was so heavy, oily and sad that one had to feel sorry for it.

Food was, strangely enough, my grandmother's main occupation. You can say what you wish about her professional choices, but her long career as a kindergarten chef has done a lot for the village and for the country. The alarmingly high number of patients with chronic stomach disorders in the district has employed the capable medical core of Bulgaria for decades. I am exaggerating, of course. Nobody would even remember Ivanka. But that's because there aren't many left who lived to tell the tale. Those who lived are still shaking and crying oily tears. Fine…I'll stop. Back then, food was food and most people would eat whatever you put in front of them. Not me and not Troj but most people. I wouldn't eat Ivanka's bloody meats, her mushy stews and absolutely not her watery, slimy rice puddings. I would eat the pancakes though, and lots of them, until my belly was swollen and achy.

Anyway, there was a way to Grandpa Troj's heart, and it was called Stalin.

My first ever artwork, if one could call it that, was a portrait of the dictator from an old photo. I also wrote the old man's name underneath, with fine lettering in silver paint with double swirls on top 'S-t-a-l-i-n'. Our grandfather cried happy tears. But it was a one-time thing that. For the most part, I would paint different kind of pictures: Stalin as a princess with an ugly tiara on his head, a hairy back and a bushy tail; Stalin eating children; a dragon vomiting Stalin (or many Stalins). "Bitch," roared grandfather and died a little. "Ye-ye, vomit Stalin, ye-ye." Oh, endless fields, full of hiding places, here I come.

5

I don't remember when Mom and Dad moved to the Agricultural Institute, I was probably just a toddler then. But I remember when I moved in. Mom and Dad's tiny home was upgraded to a bigger room in the huge employee house. I waved goodbye to Grandmother Ivanka happily, formed a steady semicircle around Dad's chest and climbed onto the motorcycle. The Vespa coughed and I moved back to Plovdiv. Plovdiv was the Agricultural Institute, peaches and gladioli, Dad's little Vespa and Mom's fragrant healing food. That was until I was ten. Then Plovdiv became something completely different.

The first I saw of the institute was the bridge and the guard's cottage. The man who lived in it proved to be a very interesting character, but I didn't care about him that day. I wanted to see the big house.

We pulled over in front of the main staircase. Dad lifted down my luggage from the Vespa and put it on the ground. Ten curious children formed a circle around my bags and me. There were no toys in sight so at least half of the children asked why. I had no answer. Then I remembered the monkey that Grandpa Slavi had made for me and dug it up from the old plastic bag that contained my dearest possessions. I lifted the monkey triumphantly above my head. The children scattered in loud disappointment. At this point, Dad turned to me, smiled mysteriously and lifted me up on the Vespa. "Are you going to show the kids your motorcycle, Iva?" I threw away the plastic bag and monkey and sat comfortably on the Vespa seat dangling my legs victoriously.

The house had two oblong floors with ten rooms and small apartments on each floor. Two long corridors separated the apartments and the big balcony. I marched into this kingdom of children in the early spring, right in the middle of the annual enforced playing outside ceremony. At the end of winter, children were ordered to abandon the long corridors in favour of green grass and walnut trees. A sweet old lady was placed in front of the grand staircase to make sure our immediate needs were satisfied and to keep the corridors free from prying children. Clotheslines and loud radios took over the balconies. Finding silence inside the building became impossible. Even the toilet was noisy. Everyone who lived on the floor used the same old bathroom and two hole-in-the-floor toilets, so bathroom manners of all residents were inspected carefully and no 'tricks' of any kind were allowed. As Fat Dana put it: "There shall be no fire crackers, no kissing and no pooping anywhere but inside the toilet hole."

It took me about ten minutes to map the institute grounds, but the refrigeration hall where our father worked wasn't easy to find. It was well hidden amongst combines, tractors and other strange machines with large rubber wings. The whole place smelled of naphtha and peaches. No wonder it became my favourite place on earth. There was an ocean of yummy food and plenty of machine parts to fiddle with and admire. Also, the boss was Dad. What was there not to love?

Needless to say, with Troj finally by my side full-time, Mom in charge of fixing people, Dad in charge of fixing wonderful gigantic machines and little me in the centre enjoying it all like a shah ruling a fairy tale kingdom; I was in my rightful place in life. But the ever-present white coats made my new paradise a little less heavenly. The institute was their world of chemicals and altered plants and us little people who lived there were a nuisance to them. Warning signs were everywhere. Everything that looked remotely delicious was labelled with orange triangles and exclamation marks. I was never concerned about that though. I had my allies. The local night guard came in handy, he seemed to know what was what. Then came our father who also seemed to know everything. Last came my own nose and highly tolerant tummy.

I had hubris back then, I thought that nothing could possibly hurt me. And remember, these were the times of the nuclear horror. Every time Soviet leaders got the crazies, nuclear exercises became obligatory. But I seriously thought I was immune.

Thing was, I was not immune. I was protected.

The first weeks after the Chernobyl catastrophe, our mother put us on canned food and bottled water. Mom had a hunch, you see. Something was 'not right with the air'. The small Geiger meter she had put on her wall at the Oncology Department the year before had been removed under mysterious circumstances. Earlier the same evening, the little device was buzzing and chirping for a whole hour. Mom hissed and cursed saying 'rotten liars' again and again at our black and white TV and forced tin food and bottled water down our throats. I wonder what would have happened if we didn't eat the tin food. In addition to chemically enhanced fruit, nuked sandwiches might have pushed my little body a bit too far.

Troj and I had few adult friends at the institute and the local night guard was one of them. Not only that, he was also my reliable partner in fruit theft. We talked about life, which is what friends do. My life was something I discussed with very few adults, but I liked talking to him. He would open with a friendly smile, a pat on the head and then move on to the existential issues. Other adults asked the same questions, but he was the only one who listened to the answers. "Hi, there, Iva! Have you figured out what you want to be when you grow up?" I would look at him, think carefully and reply highly ambiguously to allow useful input.

"Today, I believe in the following: teacher of history, though I'll be working at a school for the mentally handicapped children. Or maybe I will be a mentally handicapped child myself." He didn't judge me, just nodded and smiled.

"Okay then. Glad there is a plan."

This whole mental handicap thing was something of a fascination of mine. Every morning on my way to school, after we dropped off Troj, my father and I would pass 'Plovdiv's Specialised Secondary School'. The majority of the children at Plovdiv's specialised school for odd creatures were Romani. Somebody had written 'For Retards' under 'Specialised' on the sign, and although 'Retard School' sounded like a rare exclusive club to me, I knew that mental handicap was a broad concept for the white coats.

My class passed by that fence at least once a week. The children from 'Specialised' would flock around the fence and look at us. We would in turn slow down and look at them. At the end, we would be so close to each other that the fence would disappear. Some of them always said, "Hello!"

And we always replied, "What's up?" Nothing special to report there, apart from one or two kids that had almond-shaped narrow eyes. The teachers didn't enjoy children watching one another and saying 'hello' as much as they enjoyed children marching so they would start shouting at us waving their sticks. We would step back and the fence would become visible again.

I remember very little of my old school, only that it was very big and close to 'Plovdiv's Specialised'. I don't remember teachers' names or faces or what the building looked like inside. I do remember a girl in my class, though. She was the class bully. I must have decided to put her in my long-term memory because she did nothing but hit, kick and curse. I wasn't the type to just succumb to her bullying ways. I mean, this girl ain't leaving her donkey on the street, but my probing powers didn't work on her. She would slap me around, and failing

35

to manipulate her, I would resort to calling her names. She would kick my new backpack around the schoolyard in return. I would then write obscenities on her locker, like the not so subtle 'whore' written in red lipstick I stole from Mom. She would then move on to peeing on my new dark blue cardigan, the cardigan our Mom bought with the money she saved on work lunches. 'Saved' as in 'didn't eat' that is. That would make me angry enough to spread even worse rumours. She would retaliate in very unexpected ways. Once, she gathered a group of angry girls and half-stoned me to death on my way home.

I had enough of her at that point.

One day, I walked up to the scrawny girl who, for some reason, deliberately chose to be friends with our raging bully. "I can tell you your fortune if you let me see your left hand," I whispered. Hesitantly, she showed me her hand. I squinted, glared at her palm and made up a beautiful story about rose gardens, fancy men and a long happy life. After that, I sat in my seat and waited. Word spread quickly and soon half the class gathered in an irregular queue around me. I smiled mysteriously and allotted beautiful destinies right and left. At last, she came, bloodstains on her uniform collar, scab on her nose and her hair cut short, like a boy's. She shoved her hand in my face ordering me to 'spill the beans'. "I see a beautiful home, a lot of money and a handsome husband," I began. Her face lit up and she nodded.

"Continue, for heaven's sake!"

"But wait…what is this I see? Lightning strikes in the house, your husband dies and there's blood everywhere. He leaves you alone with triplets. Two of your children are retarded and the third is very ugly. Then you die of exhaustion before you turn fifty." The girl did not come to school for days. Then her mother showed up, grabbed me by my hair and dragged me around the schoolyard until I started bleeding.

I am not proud of that one. Not the right use of my powers.

6

Driving us to school became quite a chore for Dad and his light-blue motorcycle. We were growing by the day and he was terrified that one of us might let go of him and fall off and get crushed underneath the cars behind. There was public transportation but the institute was miles away from town and buses were always running behind schedule. So Dad sold the Vespa and bought a tiny car, a Russian Zaporozec that was bigger than a motorcycle but smaller than the then very popular East German Trabant. We fell in love with it right away. Our mother was afraid of it though. She signed crosses with her fingers leaning over the steering wheel, prayed and held the door tightly, ready to pounce. Dad explained for weeks that the car, although small, was much safer than the Vespa, but she wouldn't listen to him, she'd 'rather take the bus', she said. One day, Dad had enough of her superstitious safety rituals. He drove through a chicken farm, reached over her knees, opened the door on her side and threw a few hens onto her lap. "See, now we have dinner," he murmured. Mom let the door go. She knew that she was in for more shenanigans if she didn't stop her prayers and pagan witchery.

We could do all sorts of things in our small Zaporozec, things that were impossible to do on the Vespa. Troj and I played the harmonica, built towers, and wrestled each other. We could also talk to Dad. Although the loud buzz of the engine behind the paper-thin cover was a bit disturbing, we could still make ourselves heard. It was not easy to silence us now that we weren't sitting on the back of the Vespa. But the man had skills. "Daddy, Daddy...want...to pee...now."

"Pee then," he would say, let the steering wheel go and bring his big hands together in an improvised bowl. That was always very confusing and also quite unsafe so we would stop talking.

When temperatures fell below zero outside and inside the car, we crawled underneath our father's old fur coat that smelled of aftershave and naphtha. We lay there in the foetal position and enjoyed every second of it. I could see that

Dad was cold, but to give up the fur coat was for me inconceivable, so I silenced my conscience and thought of other things.

The Zaporozec was a pleasant novelty. But we could see that Dad was missing the shiny Vespa. Apart from his eyes tearing up whenever a rival Vespa whooshed by, there were also the never-ending sighs. One winter night, when Troj and I lay on the floor flipping through old photos, we found a whole bunch of pictures with the motorcycle in them: the Vespa, Mom and Dad on a date; Dad dressed in a stylish black leather jacket, pointy shoes and tight short-legged trousers standing in front of it; the Vespa in front of communist posters depicting communist leader Brejnev, wrinkled as an old paper bag, among gladioli flowers and flags; the Vespa and our mother. The platform shoes, the short skirt made of suede patches and the gigantic afro were just too much for us to bear. We burst into unbridled laughter, clutching our stomachs and rolling on the floor. Dad grabbed the pictures, looked through them, sighed for a good minute and a half, and put them away. We didn't see the box again until we had moved to the other Plovdiv, the one with asphalt everywhere, Romani houses, dusty forest and a vast military establishment.

There were other photos in that box: Mom at the orphanage, dressed as something resembling a clown, wearing an old grey dress, slightly torn tights, hair neatly tucked into a knot, clown nose painted with lipstick. Also pictures of our grandparents: photos of Ivanka in an improvised guerrilla uniform; Grandfather Troj as a soldier in the Spanish Civil War in 1938, barely twenty years old, with a big rifle in his hand. Grandma Ivanka's and Grandpa Troj's destinies ran in parallel to each other in all the photos. There it was, the same room, the same everyday objects, but they stood alone smiling at the camera, never together. That is how I remember them, prisoners in involuntary togetherness, togetherness that followed its own odd rules.

Dad's beauty shone through in our grandfather's face on every single photograph of him – the deep eyes, skinny but strong body and the mysterious smile. You could barely tell them apart. But it wasn't just the appearance our father carried with him, the involuntary togetherness that marked his parents' lives was a part of him too.

Mom blamed Dad for believing that love was somehow imposed on him. She looked at him as an heir to his parents' less lovable properties and values. But Mom was wrong. He left the village because he didn't want to become like them. Grandma Kerana knew that.

On one of the rare occasions when the whole family went to the mountains, our parents had a fight. It was about our father's side of the family, as usual. After a lot of whispering, our mother erupted in rampant frustration over all the insane rules and principles that were 'allowed' to govern Ivanka's house. Grandma Kerana sided with our father. She didn't defend anyone but took our father's hand, waved Mom away and said in her deepest voice: "It is a burden he carries, a burden which is not his. Do not blame him for that." Then she gathered us confused children in a corner and gave us answers. "Your grandparents down below do not hate you; they love you in their own way. Look closely and you will see." I looked at my feet wearing a pair of slippers that Grandma Ivanka had knitted and my head started spinning. The slippers were not the nicest I had, but they were beautiful 'in the way of love' – a definition of beauty often heard in the mountains.

It wasn't often our Grandmother Ivanka admitted to loving someone. She looked at love as a universal requirement for submission. But she loved us and she loved Grandpa Troj in her own strange ways. The tears she shed at his funeral came from the bottom of her soul.

The funeral itself was a different matter.

Grandpa Troj was buried with much fuss. Nothing in the absurd ceremony felt real, like he was pretending to die and the funeral was just a rehearsal. "Are you done with the medals? Good. Now we take them away."

The Communist Party seized our grandfather's death early in the morning. The bedroom was decorated with red ribbons. Three strange men carried my grandfather off to the double bed in the bedroom – a bed he hadn't slept in since he and Grandma Ivanka made Dad. He was then dressed in a suit that he never wore. People that hardly knew who he was put his medals on his chest. These were the medals that he kept in a box in his sock drawer, never to be seen or touched by anyone. Grandfather's medals: one for the Nazis dancing on his chest and forcing matches under his nails; one for bombing Nazi trains; one for saving three hundred partisans from certain death; and one for each anniversary celebrated in the name of Communism since World War II. They put on the medals in strict order. Anniversary medals were laid closest to the heart (somebody then and there decided that anniversary medals were the most important). The rest were placed on his belly. A 'comrade' stood at the door and handed out red ribbons to all mourners who came in to say goodbye to Grandpa. Another stood at the exit door and took the red ribbons back. My stomach was turning at the thought of all the fingers and chests these red ribbons passed through to mark that dead partisans belonged to The Party and not the bereaved. I guessed a thousand funerals times a hundred visitors times ten fingers equalled one million fingers and one hundred thousand soiled black funeral blouses and shirts. I ran to the toilet in the backyard and threw up. Party comrades took my reaction as a sign of patriotism.

No one from The Party came to Grandpa's burial place. I remember eating a lot of sweets, being kissed by every old hag on the way there and called 'poor orphaned girl' even though my parents were alive. And the obligatory mourners shouted themselves hoarse over our grandfather – a man they did not know.

7

Our family was starting to outgrow the Agricultural Institute residence, which at that point consisted of a room and a shared kitchenette. I felt responsible for the space being overcrowded now that I had left the village and moved in. No one complained about the room being small before I showed up with my requirements for space, air and motherly love. I had to make myself smaller.

Mom and Dad worked nightshifts at times so Troj and I slept alone. Insomnia was a mandatory part of nightshift nights. I took my temporary motherhood very seriously. We made up the sofa together, watched TV for a while and went to bed. It was up to me to choose a program that was reasonably child friendly, turn off the TV at eight o'clock, fix bedding, read a book, run back and forth with water and teddy bears, say 'Good night' to the elderly couple in the room next door (just to make sure nice things were said when they report back to Mom in the morning), brush teeth, and scare Troj to sleep if I needed to. I had a hard time falling asleep myself so I would touch and rub Troj's unbelievably soft earlobes. That made me calm but woke him up. He would protest and we would fight, but I was the mother so he had to obey.

Nightshift nights were the longest. I tried to fall asleep at the same time as Troj did; it was a game we played, 'One. Two. Sleep'. I watched over him for hours otherwise. But there were worse activities to engage in, like watching 'Козият рог' in the middle of the night. This film was not meant for me. It lasted for several long hours and showed more violence and pain than my little eight years old heart could bear. I watched how the Turks slaughtered women and burned churches, but nothing was worse than the father who carried his slain girl child wrapped in white sheets, like a mummy. The child was missing arms, legs and breasts. Missing limbs were for some reason easier to digest than missing breasts. I turned off the TV, clutching my own budding breasts and thinking that Turkey deserved the recent earthquakes and terrorist attacks, then I remembered how close Turkey was to the Sakar Mountain and Grandma and cried for everyone's sake.

41

We shared a kitchenette with a sweet old couple and took turns at the improvised stove, made up of two hotplates and a cupboard. The woman was over eighty years old, sick and very overweight, so she took her time cooking. And when she one day suddenly disappeared, the old gentleman she lived with (I believe it was her brother) became our mother's worry. Then came the earthquake, the one that devastated several towns in Turkey, and the big employee house cracked.

Mom was sitting at the table when it suddenly began to swing. She told me off but quickly realised that something else was going on. We ran out in our pyjamas and nightgowns, heard the trees sing and saw the house burst. A dream grew from those cracks – Mom's and Dad's dream of a new home.

Mortgages didn't exist in communist times so after a lot of late nights talking in loud voices, the family went on to lend land to my parents, vegetables would be grown on weekends when Mom and Dad had some 'spare time'.

Mom and Dad set the dream-fulfilment process in motion weeks after the earthquake. Troj and I were sleeping alone at least once a week.

We started commuting to the village even more often than before. Mom and Dad went to the piece of land allotted to them by the family and we stayed with Grandma Ivanka. This went on for a very long time, four summers at least. The first summer was unusually childless, and I was extremely bored. After a few dead chickens, a demolished flowerbed, a sick dog and a heavily traumatised pig, which to my absolute horror and disgust was named Iva, the family had a think and I was appointed to assist Grandma Ivanka with cooking, washing, feeding animals and caring for Troj. Mom and Dad came home at night so exhausted that I had to carry out regular health checks on them. With Grandma Kerana sick at the hospital and Ivanka unwilling to help, it was up to me to heal them.

I managed to escape Ivanka's watch every now and then to look after Mom and Dad. In order to do that, I had to somehow get to the small piece of land where they soldiered on growing all sorts of vegetables that could be sold to the state-run Communist cooperative for money or credit. The tricky part was that I had to do it without being noticed which added at least half a mile to my journey. Right on my escape route, there was a corner by the village square where old Romani women often sat with outstretched hands and toothless smiles. If you managed to ignore the cigarette smoke and the ripe smell of dust and henna, you could 'look into your soul, see spirits, and follow your fate'. Their raspy voices were strangely pleasant: "On the day you were born, dear child, a very special light was lit – a shining little star, a shiny clear path amongst the roads but a path that leads beyond the longest motorway. To be loved by you will heal the good ones and break the bad ones. An old soul knows better than to shine like a giant in the sky, visible only for those who also are old souls. Young souls you can love but not hate. They haven't lived for thousand years and nothing they know. What you learn you should pass to your two children, for they shine next to you in the night sky. Your third will, unfortunately, not live, but do not blame yourself for that."

I didn't understand all the words and was afraid of them, especially that last sentence, but every time I climbed up the cherry tree to peek over the dusty road, a strangely powerful urge to get my hand read and my fate explained to me would kick in, so I came up with all sorts of excuses to get away. That was how I began buying bread from the bakery. It took ages to walk there and the queues were long, so Grandma Ivanka was happy to grant me the task, even if it meant several hours of waiting and half-eaten loaves of bread. I walked past the neighbouring farms to say hello and ask about grandchildren's health and whereabouts, looked in at my friend Minka's to check on her new toys, passed by the house where 'coma woman' lived (the one that Eunice and her cronies gossiped to death), smelled the roses in the rose garden and entered the square hundred yards from the bakery.

There were many roads to the bakery so one could improvise to include old Romani women. I could walk past the land where Mom and Dad worked, up to the bakery through the State Vineyard and back to the family farm. Or I could walk past the church ruins and the school, through the square and back on the other side by the village store, bakery and then home. Or I could expand my route around the square but slightly in the opposite direction and past the pub where Grandpa Troj and his mates used to drink beer.

In the centre of the village park, there was a granite statue of a tall man in a guerrilla uniform. The village was named after him. He was 'Granit' – the greatest local partisan hero and our grandfather's best friend during the war. Romani women and children sat on the grass behind the enormous granite statue surrounded by candy vendors. On the other side of the park lay the village kindergarten, which was a major attraction for Romani kids, including the toddlers, with all its toys, flowerbeds and small uniformed children, all too well-behaved and cute to put up a fight for toys, country or Lenin.

43

And there I was, every chance I got, never knowing which hand was left and which was right, stretching them both in front of me, blushing and begging for more fortunes than a little girl could possibly need until they ran out of things to say and started giggling at the slightly naughty remarks aimed at me by the youngest of them.

The Romani women knew who I was long before I knew of their existence. Most of them didn't know my name, but they knew whose daughter I was. Romani women were very much aware of my father. They would gather around the family land to admire Dad's tanned body. They found excuses to hang around the fence, usually begging for food. But when our mother disappeared into the small shed to fetch bread for them, they would start yelling out horny little verses while groaning and laughing. Mom hated that.

8

In all, it took more than four years to gather enough funds to buy a new home. When that day came, we loaded the Zaz with belongings and left the institute. I yelled 'Goodbye' to Damian – the local paedophile. Damian's face twisted in a wide macabre smile and he waved back. He was happy enough to see me leave.

hey hey
little bee
come to me
let me in

hey hey
look at me
when I touch you
look at me

hey hey
little you
let my big thing
inside you

hey hey
little girl
Uncle Damian
makes you purr

hey hey
little shit
I will never let you be
if you tell on me

Damian was a dumb man, but somehow, he always found ways to persuade us to go to the bushes with him, especially the little kids. By the time I finally found a way to beat him, he had molested not only me but almost every girl between the age of 5 and 14 at the institute. I wrote down the things he said to us and made up a song. I taught the song to every little kid on the block. We would gather and follow him around everywhere he went. It didn't matter that we all got beat up and scolded by our parents, the incessant singing pushed him away from our playgrounds. All we needed to do was to start singing and he would disappear with his head held down, like a guilty child. He must have been about twenty-one or twenty-two years old back then. Decades after we moved away from the Institute, I learned that Damian fathered 'two lovely girls'.

There were no Damians in our new home in Tracia, none that I could see anyway, just ugly high-rise buildings, dusty tired woods and mud. We moved in and began refining. It took some time before the empty concrete box even resembled a home. The flat had bare grey walls with large holes here and there. The wind howled through the holes, but it was a sound that one could sing to, which Troj and I happily did. We loved this box for it was our own. Mom and Dad laid vinyl flooring everywhere. We carried the small pile of Institute furniture and placed it in the living room centre. Troj and I danced the tango to the wind music. Grandma Ivanka took the bus from the village and rolled through the door in all her glory.

Mom smiled, greeted her loudly and went to the kitchen to get earplugs. Troj and I listened happily to Grandmother's nagging this once, mostly because she was on our turf and it was pleasant to pretend to listen and then ignore her. At least, we bothered to pretend. Mom would often tire of Ivanka quickly and find excuses to shoo her out. It could be anything really, from fake invitations to a neighbour's improvised coffee party (usually put together hastily because Ivanka was there and most neighbours would do anything for Mom) to long walks for her fictional blood circulation problems. The latter idea was used that day to excuse an excursion to the old part of Plovdiv, plenty of hills and stairs to keep Ivanka busy throughout the afternoon. Cousin Mimmi and I were violently 'asked' to keep her company.

We climbed onto a crowded bus where we stood just underneath a sweaty man's armpits. Grandma Ivanka didn't like the stench so she started mumbling about the burdens of marriage and, for some reason, donkeys. We suffered the fifteen minutes' ride downtown and climbed off the bus relieved. What followed could only be described as an unnecessarily slow climb up a very small hill to the first of many churches. Cousin Mimmi and I were bored of old Plovdiv and Grandma Ivanka at that point. We moaned and dragged our feet until she got angry and sat on the narrow sidewalk in protest.

A squeaky clean white van passed by us and stopped. The driver opened the door on the right side and stepped carefully out of the car. A boy stepped out on the other side and slammed the door behind him. He barely lived to regret that. After the sudden slap came a verbal mayhem: "You dwarf of an offspring! Your mom's ass is ugly and pimply, and she is my whore, and your grandmother is my whore, and I will put my 12 inch salami up yours donkey style, so that you squeak like a pig, so you see stars in broad daylight. DO NOT do that again!"

Grandma turned her good ear towards him and froze. She couldn't hear all of it so she looked at the two of us: "What say?" My then nine-year-old cousin bit her lip and shook her head refusing to speak.

I sighed and accepted the responsibility: "The boy wants a donkey, Grandma, but it wouldn't fit in the car, it's 12 inches too big, so he gets a pig instead."

"Who is 12 inches too big?" she asked in distrust.

"The donkey," I replied.

Dad made his famous moussaka that night and everyone had a taste of his new brandy. The adults drank from a big blue bottle. We dipped our fingers in booze and licked them. Dad was happy. Dad's new home had sky-blue vinyl flooring and freshly painted concrete walls, Ivanka wept alcohol tears, and Mom was so beautiful with her huge Angela Davis hairdo. Suddenly, Dad stood up and walked into the kitchen. When he came back, he held up a bottle of golden brown brandy. "I will bury this bottle in the woods behind the house. When Iva gets married, we will drink it and rejoice."

And he did just that. He buried the bottle and we drank it many years later, when my then husband and I finally got divorced.

Tracia, the new suburb we moved to, was meant to be Plovdiv's first modern suburb. 'Modernising' in communist lingo meant building something that is large, square and populated with people who looked like soldiers in an army – uniformed and mostly concerned with communist five-year plans and 'The War Against Nature' (it did say 'against', I swear).

The neighbours planted small gardens in front of the big boxy building and Dad took care of the finest of them. Tracia started to feel a little like home.

And then came the Great Assimilation Project and the Big Name Change. Romani people were ordered to leave their homes and 'blend with us Bulgarians'. We, the 'Bulgarians', were a mixture of Armenians, Russians, natives with mixed blood, like our parents and us, the occasional Greek grandmother (all Greek people I met in my childhood were grandmothers) and one or two strangers of unknown nationality. During the Great Assimilation, Romani people were forced to change their names. Some joked about it. Some cried. Some were clever enough to change to Russian names so they 'wouldn't have to change again when Bulgaria became the 18th Soviet republic'. Everyone obeyed. Our mother spent months rewriting her patients' journals at the hospital where she worked. It was 'the most confusing, tiring and idiotic project' she had ever been involved in.

There had been rumours back in the '70s and '80s that The Party used forced labour to dig a riverbed in Sofia. It was said that our communist leader Todor Zivkov had done his statistics and realised that every other communist nation's capital had a river, so he ordered himself a river. After three years of weekends and summers of forced labour for everyone in and around Sofia, some engineers put two and two together and warned that despite its inclusion in the five-year plan, the scheduled river would drown the whole capital if water was unleashed upon it, so they forced everyone in the villages surrounding Sofia to work weekends for another three years to fill the hole. Apparently, there are still remains of signs marking where the ferry boats were supposed to cast anchor. Our mother claimed that the Assimilation Project was 'much more idiotic' than the Sofia River.

She came home exhausted, frustrated and confused about the amount of work she and her colleagues needed to do 'for no logical reason'. But being forced to gamble with her patients' lives was what had her blood boiling. All Romani patients were required to change names, but the records of these name changes were inconsistent. They were handwritten by tired, and mostly careless, office clerks, gathered in unmarked folders and delivered to her from something called 'Assimilation Office' – some strange institution she had never heard of before. These records were so below our mother's standards that she called them 'pub napkins' and swore to 'chase the bastards back upstairs' assuming 'Assimilation Office' was an actual building with people in it. It probably wasn't.

Our mother cursed and swore every day during this national catastrophe of a project that was served in her lap with no instructions or support. She even managed to get herself in a verbal argument with Grandma Kerana over it. Her audacity was unbelievable. Everybody knew that Grandma won all the arguments. The topic of that particular argument was silver linings, a favourite topic of our Grandma's. She firmly believed that 'absolutely every situation had a silver lining, even the most absurd ones'. Mom believed none of this, especially in the case of 'Great Assimilation'. She didn't win that argument, which resulted in weeks of Mom mumbling about 'silver whatnots...shit lining more like it'. Until one day, she saw it.

Mom started finding possible maltreatments in the journals, some of them quite severe. Without much fuss, she zipped her mouth shut and started making lists of things that didn't make sense to her, from medicine dosages to treatment frequencies. She got in heavy arguments with the hospital staff in charge and many times with the doctors and persisted until every prescription and treatment schedule was checked and changed to what 'made actual sense'.

I have no idea how our mother managed to do all of that and still treat her patients. Word of mouth says that her colleagues were scared of her. Nobody dared to cross her after she wished 'broken arms and legs' upon one of the doctors and the doctor fell and broke a leg. People would carefully go around her in the hospital corridors, and every time she started a sentence with 'What that man needs to learn is...' or 'You go and...', people would shout 'Noooo' and 'Stop!' I don't know if it's true, but that's how I remember it.

To this day, I fail to comprehend why 'The Assimilation Project' was forgotten so quickly. Maybe we were so ashamed of what happened that we decided to delete it from our histories, as if it never happened. But it did happen. And strangely enough, at the time, we all felt that it was the right thing to do. It was for 'their own good'.

Romani people were still called 'gypsies' back then. During pre-assimilation times, Tracia was planned to contain houses, squares, schools, parks and a number of communist centres with associated libraries and meeting rooms. But after they built the first blocks, the Assimilation Directive came and everything changed.

Ours was one of the first blocks, Block 23. We had just managed to make it ours when the beat-up trucks and horse-drawn carriages packed with Roma people and their scarce belongings, rolled in from the highway, past the military facility and into Tracia. The blocks behind ours were still empty so about half of the trucks and horse carriages rolled towards them.

There was nothing strange about that, I thought. I wasn't born yesterday so I recognised a wedding procession when I saw one. I mean, it had horses and donkeys, Romani people singing disturbingly naughty songs, dusty children in various states of undress, candy and those chewing gum bits shaped and branded to resemble cigarettes. Those could only be purchased from a toothless Romani man during weddings. But this particular wedding procession was a little too long-lasting. Days, weeks, months went by, but the Roma remained. One woman from Block 27, one of the 'poor sods' that settled in a new empty house just before the 'invasion', told us that one Roma family started a fire in the middle of the apartment and burned wooden flooring to warm up and cook food. Well, firstly, there was nothing but concrete in these apartments, wooden floors were a very expensive privilege reserved for militia-men and high-ranked Party people. And secondly, it was summer so no heating was needed. Thirdly, I would have definitely seen smoke. What was she talking about?

But something strange was going on, that was obvious.

Life went on in Block 23. I was quickly tagged as a potential artist and ordered to report at the ideology centre at my school. Troj was really good at football so he was signed up to play for the infamous Lokomotiv Plovdiv. These were the times when the now world-renowned Hristo Stoichkov was just a young rising star on the Lokomotiv Plovdiv sky, very much equal to my little brother.

I enjoyed every little task that was assigned to me at the ideology centre and Troj loved Lokomotiv Plovdiv. But talent was looked at in a different way then. There was a talent system in place and it was a system for selection of assets with potential to serve Communism. Troj and I were just like every other kid on the block, thrilled to do what was required of us and get 'pioneer' points for it. We bragged about it with pride to Grandma Kerana, whenever we saw her, but for some reason unknown to us, that particular kind of self-praise caused nothing but concern. Grandma Kerana felt sorry for us standing there disappointed to tears so she tried to explain. She looked us in the eye and said that we must complete everything we commit to and never be 'half-assing around', but we must also 'protect our hearts'. Dad heard that, mumbled that she was 'half-assing' her explanations, pulled us in the opposite direction and said that the system was designed to make 'super people' out of us, or 'uber communists', as he put it. Therefore, it was vital to use one's own brain and never grant intrusion 'deep in the soul where one's basic values lie'. That was how we started to learn the art of being ambiguous.

9

I grew up in the era of Socialist Realism – the only art genre recognised by The Party. Only art that depicted 'things as they were' was labelled 'true art'. Painting nudes was fine, but they had to be muscular and ooze ideology in the choice of colors (which meant using lots of red paint) but nothing sexual. Everything else was defined as 'anti-populist subject matter' or in my case 'mess'. My almost inhuman ability to verbalise about everything in art and music evolved from the need to argue away 'mess'.

I painted my first classical Renaissance style portrait in fourth grade. It was a portrait of a girl named Vanja, not the same Vanja from the institute but a girl in my new class. Russian names like Vanja, Tanja, Sasha, Boris, and the such, were widely popular back then. An average school class would have about four to five Vanjas and at least one Tanja.

That 'mess' of a portrait I painted was allowed to exist for about half a day.

Once in a while, leaders from The Komsomol, the communist youth organisation, would get the crazies and start organising war games. Dad had a theory on why that happened. He would say that their wives were having affairs, but I failed to see the connection. The night before I sat down to paint Vanja, some youth leaders had gathered the school children and improvised a battle on one of Plovdiv's three remaining hills. They needed a prize of some kind so they tied Vanja up against a tree in the woods earlier that day, separated the children in two teams and said that whoever got to her first would be the winner. The leaders ran around with the teams shouting and pretending to shoot until somebody's friends came up the hill with beers and they sat down to relax. The children lost interest after a while as well so they either sat down themselves or fought whoever came in their way, no matter which team they belonged to. Vanja stayed there until dark crying and wondering why on earth was this happening to her. Her father was one of the youth leaders so it didn't make much sense.

The next day, she was cleaned up and made ready for school, but she hadn't slept much and was barely holding her tears. When the Arts and Crafts Club leader told us to find a class comrade and paint their portrait, I chose her.

Needless to say, I got lost in it and more or less watched myself paint things without any rational thought interfering. My brushstrokes formed a blurred face with watery eyes, non-existent eyelashes and colorless eyebrows. In my painting, her jet-black hair was wrapped up around her face like a shawl forming a nervous knot under the chin, covering her face and neck with her ponytail. She tried to smile at me but couldn't. My thoughts got stuck in her pain and my eyes wandered up and down her body not knowing where to look. The leader was busy smoking so I took out a new tube of red paint, and feeling immense pleasure, squeezed it out behind Vanja's freshly painted devil's horns and between her legs.

Most of her portrait had to be explained away using communist lingo. "Yes, this is indeed a portrait, somewhat idealised but still…The horns on the girl's head are a metaphor for her strength and ideological beliefs. The red star on her forehead, the one that is deep and looks like a wound (it was a wound), shows that she is willing to sacrifice herself for communism." I had to repaint anyway, because 11-year-olds are not so good at explaining away blood red color lusciously flowing between another kid's legs.

Socialist realism was something that Lenin's syphilis-infected brain brought forth. Lenin valued the freedom of art highly before he fell ill and started to decompose. Somehow the decision was made and art did a violent U-turn back to medieval times. That's what was said on Radio Free Europe and our father agreed. He would listen to the pirate broadcasts as often as he could. He would lock the door, turn the lights off, sit by the kitchen table and hug the small transistor radio tightly covering it with his shirt or the obligatory summer vest. He would then spend minutes, sometimes an hour turning the knobs until he could hear the familiar voices of Free Europe.

The only way our father could explain socialist realism was as 'make-up used over bodily and mental decay'. There was nothing realistic about social realism. There isn't much one can do artistically with models like Lenin the dwarf with his thin pubic hair-like beard, fat and pimply Mao who loved cooked pork and naked little girls and the sadist sociopath Stalin. Not a single good-looking communist leader in sight. Or, as my father put it: "These communists with their fanfares and happy children, they are all like Kadafi, king of the desert, sand up his arse, all pictures of him…always water and fountains…What you see, think the opposite!"

52

Handing over my ego to the communist talent machinery was a hidden blessing, not only for the hackneyed self-belief but also for what my college teacher later described as 'the ability to keep the heart at a distance, so that it can see'. Being fed-up with flattery and the fake patina of it all comes with the wunderkind package. It humbles you. You focus on working hard and that's that. After a while, the heart learns to see the ambivalence in people, everyone's good and bad sides. I would have probably figured out the whole thing a lot earlier had I been less hyperactive.

As a child, I talked incessantly, jumped up and down and asked every question imaginable. My parents were quite fed up with my inability to sit still. There was a storm in my body and an even bigger one in my head. Thoughts of pure insanity succeeded one another. Some happened to cross the fragile boundary between unreal and real. My martial arts story was one.

"I am a judo master," I exclaimed one day and fought all the neighbourhood boys to prove it. I lost a tank-top, my left pocket lining and some hair in the process. I still thought wearing a t-shirt that said 'Judo Master' was a good idea, it kind of matched the bruises on my arms and legs and the missing tuft of black curly hair. Inner peace was something I couldn't accomplish even if my life depended on it, which it sometimes did.

After my three days' long judo fiasco, I came home and sat down for a much-needed cry. Grandma Kerana was in Plovdiv for a hospital appointment. She waited for me to get a grip, sat next to me on the floor as she always did, with her legs folded underneath her, padded my head and said: "You are a river, my child. Be the river that you are! These little setbacks are like the stones in your way and you know what a river does with stones – it floats around them like they are nothing but mere pebbles." I heard the word 'river' and proceeded with crying my eyes out.

Troj had this thing with inner peace all figured out. He understood a lot of things that I didn't. Despite that, it was he who had to bow to me, Sister Hyperactive and Superior. It was his punishment for being born exactly one year and ten months after me. His talents and accomplishments were systematically placed one step lower than mine. But his gift was, by far, the most amazing. Even I understood that. To see him play on the football field was something quite extraordinary. He was so fast that I could barely see him. The only way I could recognise him in the motion blur was by his huge grin and the unruly blond hair. He scored so many goals that, after a while, we wouldn't even bother cheering.

53

We would just sit admiring him, occasionally giving away little screams of joy. What he did to the ball was truly magic. He kicked it at a very low spin and sent it on a zigzag trajectory that was also a straight line. Despite the zigzagging, the ball somehow travelled in one direction then would suddenly change, some milliseconds before it hit. The point of encounter was so unpredictable that Troj's teammates would simply give up before the ball even hit the net.

There were at least a couple of girls watching the football games, mainly big sisters watching their brothers and the occasional cousin on a family visit. However, girls were not supposed to be interested in boys' things. Football was meant to be Dad's and Troj's hobby and chore, painting and theatre was Mom's and mine. The fact that our mother couldn't draw a decent stick figure, even if her life depended on it, didn't seem to matter much.

The categorisation of everything according to gender applied to simple everyday things as well, like the choice of toys and even the type of foods one ate. Girls were not supposed to eat heavy foods like bread and large portions of stew, which happened to be my favourite food.

Gender ruled our family's distribution of attention as well, which meant so much in our young lives. There is a lively debate still going on in my family as to who came with 'successful' me on my first art class. I don't really remember, but I'm sure whoever came was female.

That said, I could see that our dad was interested in my talents, even though I was a hyperactive creature of a different gender. He kept coming home with stretched canvases though there were none for sale anywhere. He must have made them himself. He sat in the Zaz once and drove sixty miles to a distant market to buy a tube of paint that I was missing.

He admired me with all his heart. Sometimes I would come home and find him at the table drawing, hand over the napkin or paper, afraid of being caught, with a mysterious smile on his face. Many years later, I realised that my father had a dream that now lived in me. And my grandfather Troj had the same dream before him. But my grandfather had his carriages. Dad had only me.

Grandfather Troj built horse-drawn carriages. He was a farmer with a desperate need to build beautiful things. He covered his carriages with flaming dragons and fairy tale castles with high towers, hunters, gardens, orchids, bees and beetles and lots of wild horses. They were like canvasses flying around the village neighbourhoods. Maybe those carriages were one of the reasons for my dad wanting to leave. They were everywhere in the village like a constant reminder that being an artist could only be a hobby.

I told Dad a story once. I was dying for his attention after spending two unbearably long summer months alone with Ivanka and Eunice. I had made up this tale about a lonely prisoner in a tower. The prisoner would draw beautiful pictures on pieces of paper, fold them into paper planes and throw them through the window. Dad stood up, walked to the car without a sound and went fishing.

Maybe Granit, Dad's home village, wasn't made for us either. We fled a bunch of times too, Troj and I. Summers were like long jail sentences and it was the village's fault somehow. I would go to the bakery for bread, but instead of buying bread, I would climb on the bus to Plovdiv. That crucial decision-making moment was usually quite short as I was always and utterly convinced that I didn't belong anywhere near Ivanka and Eunice. However, my timing was always lousy. Mom and Dad would come home from work far too exhausted to even yell at me so they would just put me on the bus and send me back to the village equipped with a small bag of temporarily clean clothes.

Troj was much better at this than I was. It was all about the choice of vehicle, you see. What was an angry bus trip compared to biking the forty miles to Plovdiv on a small green bike? The same day that Troj did that, Grandma Ivanka had tried to wash his little body with the garden hose. She didn't wait for the water in the wash tank to warm up enough so she told him to stand in the middle of the courtyard behind the summer kitchen and turned the freezing cold hose on him. He biked all the way home to Plovdiv late that June evening. He was covered with road dust and mud, but according to our parents, all his teeth were showing in the 'biggest smile they had ever seen'. They let him stay in Plovdiv for several days and I had to live with Ivanka's guilt and confusion. It didn't help that Eunice was there and just wouldn't shut up about the state of 'her daughter's green bike', like that mattered to anyone but her. Besides, the green bike was supposed to be Troj's anyway. It was given to Mimmi as a way to shut Eunice up in a family dispute gone violently wrong.

10

Back in Tracia, life was following its usual routine. Theatre plays for Romani children and small missions in the Romani neighbourhood constituted a large part of my communist after-school curriculum. I engaged in these activities with enthusiasm and genuine communist fervour. It was my own important mission, just as important as my mother's job at the oncology department, or so I was told.

At six o'clock in the morning every Wednesday, I stamped off to the Romani neighbourhood, terrified by the strange smells and violent screams and knocked on doors to persuade missing classmates' parents to let their children go back to school. Not infrequently, I was shooed off with a few well-chosen words such as 'Run home to your mom pussy' or 'You Bulgarian shit have top rankings in cock sucking' or 'Eime married, no school'.

Eime was a girl in my class who would often attend school only once or twice a week. Nobody knew what she was doing the rest of the time so I was sent over with a message to her parents on more than one occasion. I would go to her house, deliver the message just outside the door and run home.

One lazy afternoon, feeling increasingly bored, I decided to go back to her flat for another desperate plea. The building was relatively empty so I waved away my hard-working demons and knocked. The door was ajar so I kicked it gently with the top of my shoe. The apartment's concrete walls were hot and humid in the sun and the smell was pungent. Eime ran up and hugged me. I mumbled a bit about the school and the reason for my visit, but she didn't care. She dragged me to a room that lacked everything except a beat up rug and one half-broken chair, sat on the floor and pulled me down. I landed beside her with a thud trembling with anticipation. Eime took off the knitted grey-brown cardigan and layers of fabric wrapped to resemble an apron. Under all the fabric hid a tiny girl's body and something that looked like a pregnant belly. I stopped trembling. She had a child in her 12-year-old belly and was happy for it. "May I see yours?" she said and lifted up my uniform blouse. We lay on the floor for a while comparing bellies. Mine was a little bigger despite the baby occupying hers. Nothing strange about that, it was my friend's birthday and I had eaten a lot. My friend's mother was not very well liked in the neighbourhood so nobody showed up but me and her skinny cousin. I had eaten three pieces of cake and some stew.

Eime pointed below her belly and smiled all she could. "Here come the baby out." She spread her legs and I looked at her. I had never felt this way before, it was like the whole universe was staring at me in its tiniest, roundest, softest, most pleasant form. My body started trembling again, but I couldn't stop looking.

Soon after seeing Eime's pregnant body, I was torn out of my communist after-school activities and sent off to art classes. I might have said something about enjoying my Eime visit a little too much so measures had to be taken to keep me occupied. I don't remember whose idea that was. Dare I think that it might have been Eunice's. I vaguely remember overhearing a conversation between our mother and her. My name was mentioned several times so I pressed my ear real close to the door and listened as hard as I could. Mom was sure that I could be an artist one day and she voiced one argument after another in an effort to convince Eunice that I had gifts beyond my talent for pranks and 'perverse shenanigans'. Eunice didn't buy it. She asked Mom if she had proof and Mom said that she didn't need any. The only thing she knew was that I couldn't stop drawing. The books in our wall-to-wall bookshelves were covered with little figures and creatures, some with a striking resemblance to Ivanka and even Eunice herself. I could tell that Mom was holding back a smile as she emphasised the word 'creatures', meaning unfriendly ugly beings and not tiny cute ones. Eunice countered with a very dry, "I bet you hundred lev that she is a talentless toad compared with those nice kids that go to art prep classes."

Mom said, "I accept the bet." I'm guessing because hundred lev was a lot of money. They stopped talking and walked out of the room.

Later that week, I was marched off to an art class at the communist centre, not the local crappy place with pee stains and a library full of dusty books from the '50s but the big central one that had glass walls and its own park with statues in it. Something must have happened there, because I somehow ended up going to an art school prep class that was supervised by a real professional private tutor. That bet was wasted on Eunice though, she would rather die a horrible death than give Mom any money.

Around the same time, I started going to art classes, I discovered the military complex behind the forest that separated Tracia from downtown Plovdiv. Despite

57

my efforts to hide my budding femininity, I was visibly long-legged and big-breasted. Mom was quite concerned about my appearance so she tried to cut my hair in my sleep and force me to wear big ugly glasses. She tried, bless her, but she failed.

The soldiers were not men but boys. They didn't even wear proper soldier clothes. Plovdiv was so hot in the summer that soldier clothes would have probably killed whoever wore them. They were heavy and made of low-quality wool and synthetic industry by-products. I didn't care enough to think about that. I looked at them and saw boys. My curiosity and simultaneous disrespect were based on that observation.

These boys were very sweet individually but horrific and very dangerous in a group. When we first moved in, we tried to avoid the whole military area, because Mom said so. But after a while, we realised that we had to walk past it every now and again, as the buses in the then brand new Plovdiv suburb were very unreliable.

The first time Troj and I walked the long way around the military complex, we had waited for the bus for more than an hour. We tried to walk in the shadows of trees and cottages, but the afternoon was all too sunny and the area was quite bare. They spotted us right away. Troj stopped and started pointing at the housing area behind the ammunition barracks. I looked and saw some heads appearing through the broken window glass on the fourth floor. More and more heads appeared as the soldiers noticed us and flocked to look at me. We were far enough to escape physical encounters but close enough to hear them. Somebody threw an apple at me and shouted 'juicy little whore', but other than that, it was just horny screams and laughter.

Years later, I would watch the extraordinarily gripping film 'Иди и смотри' (Come and See) and imagine the horrors I would have endured this and other days if it wasn't for the distance. There is a scene in that film in which a Russian girl is thrown into a lorry full of German soldiers. She is passed around screaming for a while. In the next scene, she walks alone in the woods with blood running down her legs.

Good thing they couldn't reach me. And good thing Troj was there guarding.

Sometimes I would take a shortcut through the forest on my way to school but never during their breaks, because that's when they moved in large groups. It took about a month to figure out their schedule. Even if I ran into one or two of them, they wouldn't hurt me. They almost always made contact, asked for my name or phone number and tried to grab me once or twice, but I was okay with that as long as they didn't hurt me or tried to lure me deeper into the woods.

The soldiers stopped bothering me after Troj's death. Even the neighbourhood boys stopped bothering me. Sometimes I would be walking through the woods almost hoping somebody would say something, but they never did. There was once a boy who shouted things behind my back, but when I turned around, he muttered, "Oh, you are the sister…" and walked away in the opposite direction.

Our father was also becoming concerned about my appearance, but he didn't try to cut my hair in my sleep, he took me to Manasi instead. Our common dream led us to this odd man with almost inhuman hubris. Admission to one of the country's top two art schools was merciless and Manasi was the man everyone turned to. Thousands of children from half the country applied to T.L. Art School in Plovdiv but only twenty or so were admitted and at least half of them had Manasi as a private teacher.

Manasi knew art. Despite his arrogance and his almost repulsive appearance, he taught me about art. I remember every single word he ever said to me, every story, every rule. I remember his gestures as he danced around naked models and shaped lines with his fat fingers. I remember everything because it made all the sense in the world.

Manasi gave me more than words, gestures and the pain of a lost innocence, he gave me Rosie – Rosie who shared everything with me and asked for nothing in return.

I had this black and white photograph in my wallet for over two decades: Rosie and I dressed in paint overalls, with sculpture knives in hand, clay and wire in our feet. Manasi with his greyish blond beard and crazy eyes looks like a blond fat Rasputin. Awkward endless black hair and pretty dark-red lipstick on both of us girls. Rosie has her hand in my pocket. Her forearm is just about the only recognisable part of her. Her head is bent and so is mine. We look like two dogs on a leash.

Many years later, when I visited Picasso's house in France, I saw an almost identical black and white photo of Picasso, his second wife Jacqueline and a female friend.

Manasi had only sons, no daughters. Fate works in mysterious ways but not in this case. No female offspring would have survived a life shaped by this man. His sons had better odds. His oldest was my age, shy and incredibly talented. He was Rosie's first love. We didn't see much of Manasi's middle child in the studio; he lived his own life, close to his mother. Manasi's youngest son was strikingly beautiful and severely autistic.

Manasi's studio was in the middle of a courtyard behind Plovdiv's high street. The house, the yard, the emerald green hills that adorned the horizon, everything was eerily similar to the 1920s' Montmartre and therefore quite enchanting. Vintage American art magazines, an absolute rarity back then, lay everywhere. The fabric adorned model podium marked the centre of a large airy room. Beautiful models would sometimes walk around wrapped in large shawls. The round windows and the opened books with pages and passages marked for our education, everything was so refined and well thought out – the temple of a self-professed genius.

The studio bathed in the sun from early morning to late evening. Rosie and I would often sit on the steps and have our pictures taken – unruly hair, big shirts and aprons with rope around our waists – the artist's own small geishas, obedient and forever grateful. After sunset, we would light candles in the great hall. The rest of the house was drowned in impenetrable dusty and humid darkness. Manasi embraced the darkness; he lit the candles in the old chandelier, dug out an old book from his favourite pile and read to us. We formed a ring around his burgundy plush chair and breathed in the words of Cervantes' *Don Quijote*, Salvador Dali's *Manifesto*, Dante Alighieri's *Divine Comedy*, Charles Bukowski's poetry. He read in his overbearing manner, as if he ate, chewed and spat out words. Our dedicated attention was consumed with exceptional pleasure; he enjoyed it with every fibre in his being, deep down his starving soul, at subatomic level.

Winters in Plovdiv were dark and cold, but nobody cared about that in the studio. Rituals and daily routines were orchestrated and performed regardless of the weather. The snow was shovelled in big piles underneath the stairs, the fire was lit and the windows were closed. Other than that, it was business as usual. I was always freezing, though I chose to chatter teeth in the cold rather than dress in my heavy wool coat. I felt ugly in heavy clothes as my growing body felt bigger and stranger. Mountains and valleys that scared the life out of me now replaced my old body. Manasi saw that. He looked at my reflection in the window from his plush chair, his eyes met mine in the cold glass more often than I could handle. His carefully chosen comments about my disorientation and awkward movements rained over me, steered my uncertainty and prepared me for my future place in the temple.

I admired Rosie for her incredible talent. She had an understanding of the world that was simple and mirrored everything she did. Her young but experienced hands created with an incomprehensible to me precision and I loved her for it. Rosie was a delicate creature in a world of heavy concrete, and yet she was my absolute anchor.

Her body was supernaturally beautiful in my eyes. I admired and feared it at the same time. My body felt heavy and unwieldy and hers was almost weightless. But the 13-year-old Iva from the black and white photograph in my wallet is nearly as small as Rosie is. Yet thoughts of visible differences saturate most of my memories from the studio.

It wasn't long after Manasi became my tutor that I began exams for T.L. Art School. The exams lasted three long days and covered drawing, painting and composition. The last was the exam I feared the most, mainly because I hadn't practised composition as much as drawing and painting. It was all about likeness during drawing and painting exams, but composition demanded improvisation unless you had the kind of private tutor that worked at the school and knew what the theme would be. The art school teachers kept Manasi at bay by deliberately misinforming him so that their students would have an advantage before Manasi's. That didn't stop Manasi from holding a record in accepted students, mostly because he was smart enough to figure out the themes anyway. There weren't many themes to choose from in social realism. It was always something featuring workers or communist youth.

The theme given on the third day of the entry exams that year was 'Worker's Everyday Life'. That was a difficult one, because I couldn't figure out if I was meant to paint people working or people doing everyday things. I took to the middle-ground and started drawing a scene depicting a mother sending off her son to work in the fields. One thing that Manasi taught us was that a two-person composition was a poor choice because there was no such thing unless one included a third element. By a third element, he meant a person, another living thing or an object with a potent symbolic meaning, like the biblical cross, for example. I decided to put a large unidentifiable kitchen appliance in the forefront and an open door in the background. By the time I finished drawing the thing in the forefront, it was already half-time. Everyone was given a half-hour break for a quick lunch, and we were called back in for the last three hours of the exam.

I sat down and looked at what was supposed to be my composition. My whole body stiffened as it experienced a rapid plunge in a sea of fear. The forefront was vibrant with lines and color while the rest of it was more or less empty apart from two shadows, one stretching out an arm and another leaving through an opening that faintly resembled a door.

My hands were so sweaty that I could barely hold my brushes. At this point, a very large tall boy walked past my desk and knocked my water jar down. Dirty water covered the whole paper, paint started bleeding into the outlines of my figures and the composition lost whatever structure I was intending for it. I closed my eyes and prayed to every symbolic creature I could think of, to God, communist leaders of the past, pigs named Iva, apple trees and birds that I'd never seen in real life, such as the Atlantic puffin.

I opened my eyes just in time to see a teacher smiling. He wasn't there when the incident occurred so he didn't know what had happened to me. Why was he smiling? Bastard!

A couple of weeks after the exams, I went back to the school with our mother to see if my name was on the list of accepted students. There were thousands of applicants that year, and I was sure that I didn't make it, which meant that I had to aim for a different field, for example mathematics. Thinking of mathematics, I reluctantly walked over to the board to look for my name. It was right there at the bottom five of twenty-five. Rosie's name was at the top. I couldn't believe my eyes so I reached out and touched our printed names. A passing teacher smiled at me and said, "Quite a composition you painted. If it wasn't for that last work, you wouldn't have made it. Your drawings were very stiff."

11

It was soon clear that whatever money was coming into the household wasn't enough to cover our growing expenses. Following the incident with the green bike, leaving us with Grandma Ivanka became a loudly discussed last possible option. Something else had to be done.

One of our neighbours was soon leaving for Africa, Libya to be exact. Libya was then considered our 'friend nation' and people flocked to apply for work at Tripoli's new powerplant. Only a few were allowed to join the 'Tripoli crew' and almost all of them were someone's cousin or nephew. Nobody seemed aware that two-thirds of what guest workers earned abroad was taken away by the government and The Party as a way to 'even the odds'. Rich was something that only few people in the top of the communist hierarchy were allowed to be. Guest workers were somewhere near the bottom of that hierarchy.

Dad left for Libya on a cold autumn morning. I remember the feeling of growing concern spreading through my body like the vibrating strings of a whole symphony orchestra. I looked through the window and saw Dad standing there with his luggage. He put the suitcases down and stared up at us kids, yellowing forest behind him, his hands in a knot in front of his belly, his face showing nothing but fear and sadness. Troj knew right away that this sudden turn of events would make matters much worse. I started shaking, as I couldn't put my feelings into words. Troj rested the palms of his hands against the cold window and summed up the world behind the glass in one breath, "Daddy won't see me play tomorrow, for he must leave us for the desert and the Arabs' unfinished power plant." Dad lifted his suitcases and climbed on the bus with hesitant steps, his eyes still focussed on us. He slipped and fell backward. We tore loose from the window and rushed out to receive him. He was gone by the time we got there. Mom sat on the curb crying. We ran to receive her instead.

Life plunged with all its might down a brand new and lonely track. Mom devoted all her energy to survive the big and small absurdities of everyday life without Dad. Troj and I planned our waking time after her worn-out but stubborn clock. We nursed her together so she could care for us. I grew up and became a part-time mom again and Troj took care of Mom's faltering smile. My hyperactivity was put on the shelf for the time being.

I never heard Mom say it, but I know that these two long years during our father's Libya exile and the year after, the year when Troj's body died and his soul flew off, was the loneliest time in our mother's life. She fought loneliness with every fibre in her body, but loneliness won more times than it lost. When relatives sinned against us by keeping away, neighbours and friends were called to the rescue. When they left, our home became a hotel for spirits and lost souls. Tarot cards and the inevitable company of dead people kept us awake at night. There was longing and the infinite hope for closeness where living people should have been – a vacuum that she, and later I, could never quite fill.

Autumn turned to winter with lots of snow. Troj and I pretended that the small snowy hills behind the block were the dunes of Africa. We tore Dad's fur coat out of the wardrobe and breathed in his smell.

12

The T.L. Art School was a place for people of all kinds. Our painting teacher was a man with a lot of knowledge, but in our eyes, he was like a school photographer who recorded faces without thinking. He was clean-shaven, well dressed, tall and muscular, but his art, appearance, body movements and voice said nothing of importance. Our sculpture teacher, on the other hand, was just the opposite. He was old, white-haired, short and overweight, with a deafening voice and daunting vocabulary for verbal abuse.

The sculpture studio was his area of dictatorship. The models would register his instructions and change direction, position, movements and facial expressions without saying a word. We would yawn and giggle behind his back but work really hard if he was looking. He would occasionally wave his hand to silence us, give the model a sign to change pose and go out for a smoke.

The model was often another white-haired old man – a scrawny fellow named Ivan – Ivan 'sea captain, sailor and in love with Tanja'. He talked about his love between pose changes and pauses, with his cocky shrill voice as if the whole thing was a grand romantic tale, an embellished romance between two models at an art school in the Old Town of Plovdiv, among disobedient students and heavy-handed teachers. We listened to his stories. Sculpture classes were otherwise tediously boring.

Tanja and Ivan were considered alive only occasionally. For the most part, they were inanimate objects that teachers and students pulled around like organic mounds of flesh. When Tanja sat on the podium, she fell silent. She was a shy and sweet old lady with cloudy eyes and painted eyelids. I would often go up to her and ask lots of questions, but she never answered, just smiled and looked down. I wasn't sure if she participated in Ivan's romantic escapades or just let him do his thing for everyone else's amusement.

The white-haired sculptor was not involved in anything related to living people; only dead subjects interested him. Whenever the models showed signs of life, he would declare them dead with words. "Try and understand the round-shaped flesh, the wrinkled parchment-like surface. Wait with the eyes. Get the form first. Ignore the eyes."

One day, Tanja died. At first, it looked like she was practising holding her breath underwater. Then she drew her last breath and her head fell on her bare breasts. The teacher said, "Keep working. We'll carry her out afterwards," and opened the door to air the terror out. We stood motionless, hands frozen in clay that suddenly felt cold and disobedient. No sound, but Tanja's wandering soul when it left the room with a shy giggle. My gaze met Rosie's and she nodded letting me know that I wasn't the only one who heard the giggles.

Somehow Tanja's death didn't stop Ivan from smiling. "She died from love for me, the seafarer Ivan. Imagine being a girl magnet in that old age."

Every time people ask me about my art education, I end up thinking of the morgue, a place I wasn't prepared to enter at the age of fourteen but did so following the orders of our anatomy teacher.

He was a grumpy man, a retired physician with no tolerance for stress or children. Everywhere he went, he carried this big old bag full of bones. We didn't know about the bones until we started our second year at the art school. We couldn't believe our eyes when he opened his oily brown bag for the first time and we saw the greasy contents. There was a child's cranium in there. It was tiny, just a bit bigger than a tennis ball and completely white. There was something about the whiteness of it, I recall. I think he bleached it.

I must say I was intrigued. Those bones made death trivial to the point of acceptance. I looked at the child's head and thought to myself that the face of death was kind of cute, or something like that. That was before Troj died.

Manasi had piles of anatomy books in the studio. He was quite good at explaining how the bones and muscles of the body built chains and how that made them ingeniously mobile. I listened only sometimes, but it made sense. I struggled with depicting it though. I had to see the real thing. Dry German drawings of muscles were like reflections in the pieces of a broken mirror, I couldn't tell what was what.

The first time we headed towards the town morgue, I was beside myself with excitement. I couldn't stop fidgeting if it killed me. It was clearly the happening of the year. But when I saw the dead body lying there on a cold steel table, the only thing I could think of was that it had a penis. Having reproductive organs made the pile of muscles in front of me human again. Did he have children? A wife? What did he dream about? His body was slender and quite young. He must have been in refrigeration for a while though, because the color of his skin looked slightly grey.

I failed all my anatomy exams that year.

13

Art school was becoming hard. The usual blend of maths, literature, philosophy, history and physics was somewhat disrupted by the vague communist ideology that our teachers were struggling to fit in the curriculum. Contrary to what I had experienced in other places, art teachers didn't seem to care so much about communism, most of them didn't anyway. One or two were still eager to court the local communist elite. The vice principal, and one of the very few women teachers at the school, was also one of the worst. She would scream and shout at everyone who didn't follow communist behavioral criteria. She seemed to be the only one who knew exactly what the criteria entailed. My theory was that she, not unlike Eunice, would have been 'a baddy' no matter what kind of ideology ruled the day in her country. She cut my hair once or twice and punched me in the face during one of the annual communist marches. It was May 1ˢᵗ and I was smiling instead of marching with a frozen enthusiastic face. I cried the whole way home because I thought that she was going to expel me. I found Mom by the clothesline on the balcony hanging my underwear and school uniform. I was dying to tell someone but couldn't tell her, because she had enough on her mind with us smiling-when-we-should-be-marching kids.

School days were long days at Wunderkind School. All that was taught at ordinary schools was also taught to us but faster and more intense, since arts subjects covered about half of the regular school time. After the first year, we were also forced to participate in military education two times a week. I was barely coping, so after a while, I had to do what everyone else was doing – neglect some of the school work for the benefit of the arts. I settled on neglecting my maths and ideology studies, I was going to excel there anyway as I had near photographic memory and could get away with merely remembering what was drawn or written on the board. I wasn't counting on getting an obese math teacher who wouldn't write or draw anything as it meant she had to get up from her chair, and an ideology teacher who was completely out of his mind. Needless to say, I ran into some trouble that year.

There was no doubt in my mind that some of our teachers belonged in Plovdiv's Specialised School for Intellectually and Mentally Challenged. The ideology teacher was definitely one. Do you remember Brezjnev's funeral? Of course, you don't. You weren't amongst hundreds of students that were shoved into a small teacher's lounge in front of a tiny television to watch the morbid procession for two whole hours. The teachers didn't have a projector, but there were two big half-broken wooden speaker boxes available, so the ideology teacher decided to hook them to the television. The soundwaves carrying intensely heavy funeral music hit me in the face so hard that I flew backwards in the arms of an older student. He was so shocked that he didn't even notice. Everyone was just staring ahead to where the sound was coming from. Nobody knew what was going on. I thought that the world had ended and I teared up. There were other kids crying around me. The vice principal walked towards our corner of the crowd and patted one of us on the head saying, "There, there, it's okay to cry, child; he was our beloved leader."

"Who that?" I stuttered without thinking.

The vice principal's mouth started foaming while she was pressing words through her teeth: "Who said that?"

The year our father was scheduled to return from Libya was rapidly approaching. It was almost winter, and I was really starting to like art school, despite all the madness. Gifts from Dad kept coming in the mail, and although I didn't want them to stop coming, I really wanted our father back. The gifts were amazing though. There were fancy white jackets, tight light-blue jeans, little red purses with pearl buttons on them, plenty of jerseys for Troj and a pair of real football shoes, not the kind they issued at the club. There was also lots of chocolate, not the tasteless grey kind that didn't have any cocoa in it but real milk chocolate with big hazelnuts.

I don't remember what else came in those packages from Dad. There must have been gifts for Mom. Our father liked giving her presents; it made him happy. Now and again, he would run out of money to get her gifts so he would pick flowers or bring her seemingly random things he'd found somewhere. She always made use of whatever Dad brought her.

Before Dad went to work in the desert, we would wear the same things that all other kids in poor families wore. The few stores that sold children's clothes were all full of dark green, brown or grey clothes that didn't fit very well. We had to wear uniforms most of the year, so nobody owned a lot of clothes. We didn't even have a separate wardrobe. Most of our family attire fit in one big wooden cabinet, Dad's clothes on the top shelf, Mom's underneath, one drawer for me and one for Troj. The only clothes we really needed were underwear, dark blue cardigans to put over our uniforms, winter coats and summer clothes. Good summer clothes were the thing that all kids truly desired, but there were none that were in any way fashionable. That was problematic for me. Now that I was an aspiring artist, I needed to look like somebody who didn't belong to the large dark-blue or grey masses. I made sure both our parents knew that very well and had just about zero understanding of – or interest in – their, and by proxy, our dire situation.

Dealing with Troj's death has forced me to persuade myself that I wasn't a selfish child, but evidence to the contrary is piling up as the memories start coming back. I remember screaming at our parents, demanding funds for a very expensive school trip abroad. They had just about enough money to buy us food and soap. Soap was cheap so when facing hard choices, our mother would use it instead of dishwashing liquid and laundry detergent. I also remember crying my eyes out for not having a 'nice jacket' to wear in the fall or on 'cold summer nights'. There is no such thing as cold summer nights in Plovdiv. Plovdiv is probably the oldest city in Europe and one of the reasons why it has survived for so long is the fact that it is surrounded by hills and mountains. In the summer, Plovdiv turns into a cooking pot with temperatures soaring up to 40–45 degrees Celsius. It is unbelievably hot and cold winds or even light summer breezes are usually very welcome, especially in the evenings when everybody is sick and tired of the scorching sun.

The irrationality behind my reasoning didn't matter to me that day when I was demanding a jacket. Troj heard the racket, popped his head through the door, laughed and ran out to play. Our parents were trying to argue with me while I was screaming at them: "I don't care, I really need a nice jacket!"

Mom sighed and said in the calmest voice she could muster, "Where do you expect us to find that jacket? On the street? That's not how it works and you know it." It made sense, and I did know very well how things worked, but admitting to that would mean accepting that I would never ever have a jacket. Our parents didn't have any money and, in my childish obsessed mind, that was unfair to ME.

Grandma Kerana had a saying: "If you don't have food on the table, you have one problem. If you have food on the table, you have a thousand problems." I was creating at least one-third of those problems just by not wanting to accept things as they were.

Thing was that I was allowed to be selfish, not because it was somehow permitted (it really wasn't) but because our parents always found a way to get us what we needed. I knew that I would get that jacket if I threw a fit, because they would be thinking of that the whole week until an opportunity to solve the problem presented itself. And there was always an opportunity, even if it meant going to Africa.

That week, they couldn't think of anything else. Mom borrowed a fashion magazine from a neighbour whose husband was a sailor at a freight ship. It was a German *Burda* magazine and the neighbour had more than twenty of them. Lucky woman. *Burda* magazines were a real foreign treat as they contained so much information. Apart from the clues to what was going on fashion-wise outside the Balkans, they contained something much more desirable – dozens of sewing patterns for garments of all types, from shirts and trousers to summer dresses. Mom ordered me to sit next to her and look through the patterns. She would suggest one after the other instead of the jacket I so desired.

A jacket is a really hard thing to sew and our mother was only an oncologist who learned how to sew at an orphanage while desperately trying to remodel her tiny wardrobe. She wasn't up to the task, but I didn't understand that at the time. I thought that she had a thing for cardigans that year and I hated cardigans, especially the ones Ivanka knitted for me. The *Burda* cardigans were slightly better, but they were all a version of the typical bulky '80s' cardigan, and I looked 'huge' in those.

A day or two after the jacket related screaming and shouting, just driving by the Friday Open Market, our father spotted a tiny hole-in-the-wall shop with pieces of leather hanging on wires over its entrance. Dad parked the car, walked up to a short skinny Romani man and asked about the leather. What he wanted to know was if the man had anything bigger than what was on display. The shopkeeper shook his head. Dad sighed and walked away. Thirty seconds or so later, he heard the man calling. Dad walked back, slightly annoyed and told the man that he needed something for a small leather garment, 'no point in shouting' if the man didn't have what he needed. The man started throwing flattering comments about Dad's appearance thinking that the leather was for him. Dad told him it was for a child and waved goodbye again. "Not so fast," the shopkeeper shouted and added that he just remembered a big piece of red pleather in the back. He 'acquired' the piece from a factory that manufactured car seats for the Romanian car manufacturer Dacia.

Dad laughed out loud nodding and saying, "Yeah, right…just like that, huh? I bet it cost a little less than a cigarette or two." The man didn't like the comment, but not wanting to miss the rare opportunity to sell something he probably got for free, he offered Dad the pleather. After hassling for a while, Dad 'took it off his hands'.

Mom started behaving in all sorts of strange ways. She would send us off to bed early and check on us every ten minutes or so until we were asleep. Sometimes I would wake up in the middle of the night to peculiar rattling sounds. It scared me a little, but I was hoping it was the neighbours. On my birthday, in the beginning of July, our parents presented me with this beautiful red pleather jacket that was exactly what I wanted. It had everything: a shiny silvery zipper, small metal buttons that Dad had found at a nearby shoe factory, two very well placed pockets and a collar with a button for windy weather. I was ecstatic and couldn't stop shouting and jumping up and down. They looked really pleased and quite proud.

I would wear that jacket day and night, through the entire summer, despite it being so warm that I was constantly just about to faint from dehydration. I made our parents regret going through all this trouble just to see me almost kill myself for fashion. I was still wearing the jacket when our father left for Africa.

One of the things Dad sent us in one of his packages was a real stereo. It was silver and black. It may have been a gift for Mom, but we took it for granted that it was ours. I never let Mom use the stereo, although I knew that it would help her fight the loneliness she was feeling after Dad left. It was quite clear that I was becoming just as selfish as the rest of the art students in my school.

Being arrogant came with the territory. The minute my name appeared on that art student admission list, I became a member of the town 'Intelligentsia' – a kind of Eastern European cultural aristocracy that had quite a population in the capital but only a couple of hundred people in a small town like Plovdiv. Being part of the Intelligentsia was exciting. The membership came with a higher status in society along with a wunderkind label. The attitudes towards me changed altogether. Instead of shouting at me, adults started listening and nodding with approval at every sentence that came out of my mouth. It was all very strange, very sudden and a little scary. But I'm not saying that I didn't enjoy it.

Even in its first year, art school offered a variety of experiences that I wasn't expecting. I had a vague idea of what the classes would be like. The art I was surrounded by gave me some clues as well, or so I thought. Our father was a big fan of Rubens, and I liked the work of William-Adolphe Bouguereau, although I had no idea who he was and couldn't spell his name if my life depended on it. My knowledge of the world outside our little country was so limited that I imagined that Rococo and Neoclassicism were styles that were still taught and practised in other countries, Italy and France for example. The religious motifs and the lack of a worker life perspective confused me somewhat, but I didn't expect to understand all things art during that first year of art school. Nevertheless, I expected to learn everything I needed to know in order to create works like Bouguereau's but maybe with a hint of worker life perspective.

I became more and more involved in the life of the city. I started attending concerts and university lectures alone, which was unheard off even for a roughly independent teen. The books I read changed genre altogether, from turn-of-the-nineteenth-century adventure novels to American classics and Chinese philosophy. Although Chinese philosophy didn't make much sense to me at the age of fourteen, it certainly did at the age of sixteen. In between came *Siddhartha*, a novel by Hermann Hesse written in 1922, which is probably why it slipped through the cracks at the Cultural Censorship Committee; J. D. Salinger's *Catcher In The Rye*, which made me wonder if capitalism was really that different from the society I was living in; Robert M. Pirsig's *Zen and the Art of Motorcycle Maintenance*, and a large number of peculiar sci-fi novels written by Bulgarian and Russian authors. When I read *Zen and the Art of Motorcycle Maintenance*, I couldn't help but think that our father would fit perfectly in that story. His love for the light-blue motorcycle and his way of discussing the concept of quality, a term he conceived as undefinable, just like the main character in the book, was all so remarkably similar to what was written in the pages in front of me.

I was reading books that were never mentioned in any literature reviews or classes and finding more and more obscure things to read became an obsession. I hid the books around the flat and read everywhere and all the time, even in school during art classes when teachers went out to smoke. Then the invitations started to come. I had never been invited to coffee before. The only coffee I had ever had was with our mother on rainy afternoons, whenever other company failed to show up.

The first afternoon coffee I attended was at Rosie's house. Rosie's mother was an opera singer and her frequently present friends were dressed in colorful clothes, talked about audiences in Prague, Milan, Berlin (not the boring Berlin on this side but the 'hot one' on the other side of the wall) and discussed poetry. Rosie's father was a mathematics professor who seemingly disliked the company her mother was keeping.

People like these didn't exist in my world, they were a life-changing novelty and, although I couldn't add much to the high-society conversation, I felt like a new and better person sitting there sharing coffee and tasteless soggy Ivanka-style cake with them.

Another amazing thing my friendship with Rosie had to offer was a marvellous crazy neighbour. Not the drunken type that came by our flat for the occasional hand-out but the interesting, theatrical, over-exaggerated and totally mad kind. The neighbour was a retired member of the Intelligentsia so people seemed to tolerate her madness out of respect. She would wait until Rosie and I were alone in their house and knock on the door complaining about low blood pressure that could only be cured by a glass of 'that lovely cognac your father brought from Vienna'. The cognac was long gone as she had drunk it on her four or five previous unannounced visits, but she wouldn't give up until Rosie fed her something or gave her a glass from the liquor cabinet. If it was somebody else asking for a drink like that, I would have thought 'what a wino', but her taste was refined. If the only available alcohol in the house was cheap vodka, she wouldn't drink it but smear it on her stomach claiming it 'did wonders for her achy joints'. Stomachs were not joints but who cares about pesky details when a mad person is performing.

On one of these unannounced visits, the skinny aging actress gave us one of her 'famous' lessons in makeup. She was 'good at makeup and men', she said, gathered all the makeup in the house and dumped it in the middle of the kitchen table. I had never seen so much makeup in my life. I didn't use any until I was about twenty-six years old and our mother used only eyeliner and sometimes lipstick. The mad neighbour started showing us how to make our eyes bigger, which we hardly needed since both of us had big black eyes. She didn't listen to our protests and force-painted our faces until we both looked like something out of a '70s' Uzbek opera. Don't misunderstand me, we didn't lack appreciation for the Uzbek arts, we just couldn't see any beauty in what our old televisions did to the images from Uzbek TV.

At some point, the neighbour started talking about the mental institution she spent most of her retirement days in. "Like that's unusual," Rosie whispered sarcastically while cleaning the makeup off her face. The woman marched around the room waving an embroidered silk handkerchief like she was dancing Flamenco.

"Do you want freedom and men, my dears?" she asked. "Or women for that matter," she continued, laughing. "It's all there, you know, the only place where you can have freedom, men and women licking your pussy as much as you want…the only place where you can have all that, no questions asked, is called t-h-e l-o-o-n-y b-i-n. It's a fucking heaven!"

It was the best afternoon of that year.

Intelligentsia had its perks, but the higher I climbed up its pyramid, the closer I came to the kind of men every girl on the planet should avoid at all cost.

14

According to Radio Free Europe, the winter of 1983 and 1984 was an unusually hot winter in the US, so hot that scientists all over the continent had to rethink available research and gather new data. It was the winter before Dad was supposed to come back from Libya, and for us, it was a particularly cold and snowy one. Dad was not the only one missing from our lives, we had also lost Grandma Kerana. We felt completely alone in the world, Troj, Mom and I.

Grandma had been ill for a while. She started coming to Plovdiv, because she was getting treatments at the hospital where our mother worked. The thought that it was Mom that had treated her hit me one day about two years ago. I didn't connect the dots at the time, thinking that she was getting cancer treatments at the hospital and that was that. The fact that it was exactly where our mother worked didn't enter my head until much later. It had been unbearable for Mom to watch Grandma wither like that. It broke my heart to think that it was she who administered Grandma's treatments on the cold steel table, watched her fall into a near coma trying to stay calm and strong, listened to her uneven breath while the invisible rays were ravaging her body. I bet she prayed a lot, mumbled quietly in the corner of her monitoring room leaning against the yellow wall, too scared to look through the glass, waiting for the treatment to end.

It wasn't the first time Grandma had been ill. The story of her other illness, the one that ended with our mother and two of her siblings living in an orphanage, is a shady one to say the least. I sometimes wonder if our mother and her siblings were taken away because of something that happened or something that our Grandma did. That kind of thing happened on a regular basis back in communist times. Journalists and even regular citizens that said the 'wrong' things or asked too many questions would end up in jail or have their children taken away, even the babies. There were plenty of bored childless wives of high-ranked officials and military men to take care of the cute babies. The rest of the children were sent off to orphanages like Mom's.

There is nothing in the information I have about our grandmother that would point to any indiscretion on her part, except the fact that she was an odd woman in the context of communism and most of her life story was either unknown or told and explained in ways that made us suspicious.

We knew very little about her. I am not sure if our mother knew even half of her mother's story. For one, she was an old lady that lived with a man that wasn't her husband. That was so unusual and frowned upon that it often felt like she was the only woman in the country to have such an arrangement. I didn't think about it much since I absolutely adored Grandpa Slavi, but it was a very strange thing indeed. Another strange thing she did was talk to the plants in her garden. She wouldn't hold speeches, nothing like that. She would speak to her plants individually while watering them, and she would tell them what to do to 'grow better'. We would sometimes laugh at her strange ways, but her plants grew like nothing I had ever seen before. After a while, we had no reason to laugh.

Troj and I were also told that our grandmother went to school for three years only. 'Which school?' we would ask because there wasn't any in the village. Our mother would sigh and say 'they lived in another nearby village called Kostur'. I knew all about Kostur and it wasn't very different from Glavan where she had her house and garden. I also knew that our mother was the only one of her siblings not born in Greece, which is why she didn't speak any Greek. That meant that our grandmother was an adult when she came to Bulgaria. So, 'Where did she go to school then?' No answers were given.

Another thing that didn't make sense in that whole Grandma's education story was her knowledge of things that could only be learned in a big city college if one was an exceptionally clever and curious student of foreign cultures. She would sometimes talk of 'wabi-sabi', something Troj and I thought was a word from a made-up language she crafted by the fire on cold winter nights. It turned out to be a concept in Japanese aesthetics representing a world view centred on the acceptance of transience and imperfection. According to wabi-sabi, beauty is 'imperfect, impermanent and incomplete.' I learned that almost by an accident, more than twenty years after her passing.

I took my masters in science and not art, for reasons I may, or may not, mention here. While studying for one of the cognitive science classes, at a nearby cafeteria, I ran out of paper to write my notes on. I went to fetch a napkin, and when I went back, I saw a bundle of articles on the floor. Somebody must have dropped them, I thought, and started looking around for whoever was missing a bundle of papers. Everyone was sitting down in peace with themselves, so I put the bundle in front of me, sat back down and continued to write my notes. I didn't pay much attention to the articles at first but became curious after a while. I started reading whatever I could see without disrupting the order of the articles, carefully lifting page after page. And there it was, *wabi-sabi* 侘寂, beautifully written in neat lettering. I couldn't read the whole article, but it all made amicable sense. Grandma would often talk about beauty being 'transcendent' and 'imperfect'. She would send us off to her garden on errands, asking us to find tomatoes or apples that were 'perfect'. We would look for the perfect apple but could never find it. All of the fruit had little dots here and there, uneven coloring or unusual shapes. We would bring her the one we thought was 'the most perfect', but she would only say 'There is no such thing' and send us back out.

How did she know about wabi-sabi and all those other things that sounded like made-up words she crafted by the fire on cold winter nights? I may never know.

Another story that didn't make much sense to us was the one about her moving from Kostur to Glavan and starting her life anew. She 'built it up from nothing', we were told. That couldn't be right, I thought. I knew that our mother's family wasn't without means back then. When I asked about the move to Glavan, I was told this strange story: A lightning struck the farm in Kostur when our mother was about seven. The lightning hit Mom and ignited the carpet she was sitting on. A couple of villagers saw the smoke and came to the rescue. One of them, the village teacher, went in the house and found Mom unconscious. They were so busy trying to revive her that they couldn't tend to the fire quickly enough. The whole place burned down. Mom said that she could still hear the animals scream from the burning barn (I thought she was unconscious but pardon me). The village teacher was the one that came up with the idea to 'ground her', meaning bury her in the ground so that the electricity would be 'drawn away' from her body. Somehow that was a genius idea and she miraculously survived. Mom lifted the hair on the back of her head and showed us a bald spot 'where lightning hit her'.

At first, I thought that it all made sense, especially after seeing that bald spot on the back of Mom's head, but the older I got, the more I didn't trust the tale about Kostur. The part where the village teacher buried her in the ground sounded less and less scientific the more I learned about physics. Besides, it happened in the middle of winter when the ground up in the mountains was frozen solid and impossible to dig in. Also, the way they all referred to their house as 'the farm' made me suspect that they weren't poor.

Apart from the suspiciously miraculous faux science behind Mom's recovery, the main reason for my doubts was something our Aunt Dora mentioned once. Apparently, they owned a store, a kind of old-fashioned supermarket that would sell anything anyone may need. It was the only store in the region and Mom's family owned and ran it. So, what happened with the store? How come a store owner like our grandmother became so destitute that she had to move to a different village and start from scratch? There was obviously a lot more to that story than we were led to believe.

Our mother was born in July 1948, or so she claims. According to her passport, she was born in August that year. All of her relatives called her Dinche, which I've been told is short for Kostadinka. That is not her name. Her name is Dena. We were also told that our grandfather died of pneumonia after being caught in a blizzard. That happened about eight or so months before the farm in Kostur burned down. In my mind, that sounded like a bit too much tragedy in that short period of time. Also, being helpless and giving children away to orphanages was not typical of the way our grandmother behaved. She was a woman of strong character, high morals and steadfast principles that she followed without exception. And yet Ivanka was the one with the medals and Kerana was the one with the mysterious illnesses, orphan children, dead husband and burning houses. Somebody was definitely lying to us.

It turned out that we weren't exactly lied to but rather not given the full information. There are many pieces missing and the keepers of those secrets have all died.

The farm and store that our Aunt Dora was talking about were in Greece. When Grandma's family moved across the border to the Sakar Mountain in Bulgaria, they were forced to abandon everything. Our Grandpa Atanas was a highly educated military man, and before they had to abandon their land, he supervised rescue missions. Grandma helped him by running an improvised field hospital. Mom wasn't sure if it was a hospital, it could have been a tent. It didn't matter. She pulled migrants out of holes in the ground not being able to tell their gender or age, because of the 'state they were in'. She bathed them and made clothes out of whatever fabric she could find, fed them and sent them on their way. Nobody knows where she sent them. It all happened in Greece and there were no medals issued. Some of these migrants and prisoners of war might have been Japanese, we assumed.

The story on Grandmother Ivanka was much more consistent with the dominant communist worldview back then. It was also a story often told and chronologically complete, with no missing decades here and there. Grandma Ivanka was humble about her medals, but even her passport contained an attachment that said 'Hero Card'. She had the biggest pension of all the neighbours, because of her 'hero' amendment. I couldn't, for the life of me, figure out what she might have done to deserve all this money and honour. I asked her many times, but since I couldn't muster asking her respectfully, I ended up with stick marks on my legs and a very dry 'Wouldn't you like to know'.

It really bothered me that she wouldn't tell me. I kept asking myself and occasionally Troj: "If Ivanka is a hero, what is Grandma Kerana then?" Troj didn't have an answer, but he knew how to ask respectfully.

One day, he caught Grandpa Troj in a good mood, relaxing under the vines with a beer, sat on his knee and said: "Gran'pa, how come Grandmother has a hero card in her passport?" Grandpa was only happy to tell his favourite grandchild the story of Ivanka's heroism.

They were married young. Almost immediately after the wedding, Grandpa left for Spain to fight Franco. "Your grandmother was alone, so she had to learn how to live with the rest of my family," he said with a mischievous smile on his face. He had a sip of his beer, his expression turned serious and he continued. 'Aunty Eunice' (Aunty with a 'y'? Grandpa, please!) was born after the Spanish war, just before Bulgaria became officially involved in World War II on the same side as Nazi Germany. Grandpa didn't have time for his wife and newborn child, because the fascists were everywhere and 'he had to do something'. He joined a large brigade of communist partisans and headed for the mountains to fight fascists and sabotage freight trains headed for Hitler's Germany. His wife became part of the underground movement that protected him and his fellow partisans whenever they were in the village for supplies or weapons. Most of the families in the region had at least one family member in the partisan brigades so they all joined in building a chain of underground bunkers and other improvised hiding places. Our house had one in the cellar, behind a heavy wardrobe that was otherwise full of vintage wine. Quickly opening a wall full of heavy bottles on solid wood shelves would have been impossible for one person so they painted the inside of the bottles and glued them to the shelves to make them seem heavy and full of wine.

At this point, Grandpa Troj took a long pause, now and again taking small sips of his beer. Troj wasn't sure if there was more to Ivanka's heroism so he said: "Was Grandma being your helper then? Was being the helper also being a hero?" Grandpa waved his hand in an inpatient gesture, as to say 'whatever you say, boy' but then realised that Troj wasn't judging anyone, just wondering out of sincere curiosity. He made himself comfortable on the low wobbly chair and continued talking.

"No one was just helping, namesake. Once you became a member of the resistance, you risked your life every day. Your grandmother played a very dangerous game pretending to support the fascists during the day and hiding partisans and Jewish people during the night." Troj's ears perked somewhat.

"Why did she hide the Jewish people, Gran'pa? Were they part of the…the reson…stains too?" he asked with anticipation. Grandpa Troj laughed.

"Nah, but they were in danger of being killed in Hitler's camps. We had no choice but to hide them too. We didn't give one single Jew to Hitler, boy. Not one…not even an old wrinkly one. The Rumanians sent hundreds of thousands. Did you know that?" Troj shook his head more than once just to make sure Grandpa understood that he had absolutely no idea of such things.

It was late and Grandpa was getting hungry. His son was cooking something that smelled absolutely heavenly so he put his grandchild down and headed for the kitchen.

The rest of the story about Grandma Ivanka's heroism came unexpectedly, without us asking for it.

It was a summer evening, roughly a year after we heard about the Resistance. One of Grandfather Troj's nine siblings, his oldest sister, was visiting. I saw her get off the bus in the centre of the village. I was doing my usual rounds about the Roma hangouts when I heard the bus come in and saw her wobbly figure descent upon the village. I immediately dropped whatever prohibited thing I was doing and ran as fast as I possibly could to alert Troj. I found him hovering above some rusty tractor remains. "The Bearded Lady is here," I whispered almost completely out of breath.

"No way," Troj said and started running towards our house. I hated when he left me behind like this.

By the time I arrived at our front yard, I was more or less crawling. Bearded Lady wasn't there yet. Dad was already setting the table and the neighbours were alerted to her presence. She didn't really have a beard, only a dozen long hairs sticking out of her chin, like grey needles that made the bottom of her face look like a balding hedgehog. Her voice was also unusually low for a woman. When Troj asked me what pirates sounded like, on one of our nightshift evenings, I told him pirates sounded like Dad's bearded aunt. He knew exactly what I was talking about.

Bearded Lady was the most outspoken person that existed on the planet, we were all sure of that. She would say whatever was on her lips, no matter how awkward it made everyone feel. If anyone reacted, she would say: "Oh bu hu, I'm too old to care about your feelings." In tact with verbally insulting half of her family, she would sing songs that made our mother wrap her arms around our ears. I didn't like that at all, my ears were blocked and I couldn't hear anything. So whenever Bearded Lady opened her mouth to sing, I would stick my fingers in my ears on my own accord. If our mother's face expressed anything other than delight, I would take my fingers out slightly so I could hear what was sung.

One song I heard her sing that night, with my fingers half-stuck in my ears, sounded a lot like an old folk song I knew. Most of the verses seemed rather innocent. It was about a conversation between a mother and her daughter who was looking for a husband. The mother was giving advice. In verse after verse she was telling her daughter to 'go into the world' and find herself a boy. 'Go seek a Jewish boy...go seek a blond, blue-eyed boy' and so on. The daughter failed in all the verses so at the end of each verse she would state her explanations for failing to find a husband. Safe to say, it was a very racist song. Some of the boys weren't exactly blessed with a pleasant appearance, some had the wrong nationality and some were just 'so damn dumb'. In the last verse, the mother encouraged her daughter to seek a Roma boy. That's where it got really interesting. "Let him squeeze you between his strong legs, taste his salty skin, drown in his..." That's when our mother discovered that I was eavesdropping.

Later on, when Bearded Lady got tired and a bit drunk, we were allowed to return to the table under the vines. Mom cleared some of the leftovers, gathered a large bowl for the dog and ordered us to feed it. Troj went reluctantly, and I stayed curled up on a small, three-legged chair beneath the table, listening. Grandma Ivanka returned from feeding the animals and sat down to rest her legs. Dad's aunt started pointing at Grandma laughing. "This one...this one..." she said between outbursts of laughter. Ivanka froze and her face went white as a sheet. Something nasty was definitely coming. "This one has herself a hero card.

Ha ha! Did you tell them what happened? Thanks God Almighty for your peasant simpleton sense of humour!" Suddenly, she stopped laughing. The corners of her mouth went down like something was pulling on them. She looked completely serious and a little scary.

Troj returned from feeding the dog, and realising Bearded Lady was saying something important, he punched me in the arm as to say 'That's for not calling me over when it got interesting.' He tried to sit on my knee, but I pushed him to the ground.

"It was that simpleton sense of humour of yours that saved us all. I was not expecting them so soon. Katarina saw the fascists gather outside the old church. It would have taken them twenty minutes at least until they got to this neighbourhood and then they had to look. I thought we had more time." She stopped again, looked into her shot glass and started spitting on the ground beneath her chair. Troj grabbed my leg in fear. This time, I let him hold me, he was clearly scared. Bearded Lady spat a dozen times stuttering 'that small-cock fat little weasel'. Dad took away the bottle she was holding. His brandy was too precious to be waved around like that.

She started wrestling our father for the bottle, but that match was short-lived. She was too drunk, and Dad was about ten times stronger than she was. Mom, the peacemaker, got involved just in time. She handed Bearded Lady a beer and shouted with a nervous laugh, "Everybody relax!" Grandma Ivanka thought she was out of the public eye, said 'phew' and got up using Troj and me as support.

"Sit your ass back down!" the huge beer bottle shouted.

"That fat small dick weasel Ivan was a traitor. I should have known. I should have. He was such a weakling in the sack, I could snap him with my little finger. He betrayed us and led them right to the cellar. We could barely manage to put the wardrobe back against the wall. They marched right over they did...the shitty vermin. And that weasel led them." And she spat again, 'Ptui'. It wasn't pretty.

"This Ivanka here...she was the lookout. She was caught by surprise too. They must have marched with rocket speed, the vermin. She was using all the flattering fascist phrases she knew; we could hear her almost lose her marbles a couple of times. Boy, was I scared to my chattering teeth. They were shouting and getting real close. There was a child just behind me in the hole. He dropped a toy and the fascist vermin heard the sound." She paused again, but this time for the dramatic effect. "This Ivanka here lost her mind completely, and the simpleton humour that I was talking about, kicked in just in time. 'Cat! The cat!

There is your four-legged partisan right there,' she said. That's exactly what she said, to the word." Grandma Ivanka was smiling a small careful smile.

"The vermin slapped her in the face, kicked her around for a bit and left with that fat weasel limping behind them. I loved seeing him decapitated...the shit!" Ptui.

"Were you okay, Grandma?" Troj asked.

"Oi, I thought you'd gone to bed already," Bearded Lady shouted. "She was all right. I've seen worse."

So, that's how Ivanka got her hero card. It took time to process that story, especially the part about Ivan the Weasel. We imagined his fat body lying on the ground with his small penis in the air and no head to speak of. We couldn't sleep for a week.

Our personal hero, Grandma Kerana, had died recently. We thought of her a lot during that first year after her passing, but then, we started behaving like she was still with us, no less or more than when she was away in her house in the mountains refusing to travel because 'traveling was a brutal thing to put one's identity through'. She was a woman with principles that made more sense than anything they taught us in school, and as long as we followed her principles, she was there, just above our balcony, lingering in the autumn mist.

Accepting her death was, otherwise, too painful.

But following her principles didn't come easy. Truth was, adapting to the structured life offered by Communism, however shallow and full of lies, was easier than trying to understand and follow high moral principles. As a child, I would repeat the words she said, most times just to please our mother, but I can't claim any understanding of their meaning. 'Greatness travels quietly' was one of many sentences she frequently spoke. It was made up of three words and these words didn't fit together in my mind. Who does she mean by 'Greatness' exactly? And how about 'quietly'? Why not noisily? For decades, I thought that she meant something in the style of that old saying, 'An empty room echoes.' Most nations have that saying in different forms and metaphors, many of them involving empty jars and coins.

Many years after I left Bulgaria, was married, divorced and became a mother, I had an epiphany.

My daughter Saga and I were taking our usual Sunday stroll around King's Garden in Stockholm when she suddenly cried out. She had been stung by a bee and her little toe was hurting where it had left its stinger for the first and last time. We had to sit somewhere so I grabbed her in my arms and went into the Culture House Library at Sergelstorg. Luckily, the bookshop attendant had some band-aids. I wrapped one around her little toe, and she calmed down. Not long after I put the sandal on her foot, she ran away and straight into an entrance marked 'Quiet Area'. I hadn't been to that part of the Culture House so, instead of chasing her and calling her back, I said 'sssh' and followed her in. It was a children's books and comics library with a separate area for play, full of activity panels, interactive games and toys. I sat down and watched her explore the library. She brought one book after another, put her finger to her lips, said 'sssh' and placed them in front of me. One of the books was so heavy that she almost ripped the cover off dragging it to where I was sitting. It was Shaun Tan's *The Arrival*. I took it off her hands and opened it carefully. I had never seen anything more beautiful in my life. Gently drawn soft images appeared and a story unfolded in front of me. Beautiful faces, cities that looked like something out of a dystopian black and white film but much more fantastical, and small cute magical pet creatures were speaking to me without words. It was a picture novel without any text apart from signs and notes in a made-up language. I waved to Saga. She dropped whatever she was carrying to add to the pile, came and sat on my knee. She watched me turn page after page without a sound, with her little mouth half-open and her tiny hands clinging to my arm. We sat like that until a very loud speaker-voice announced that the library was closing.

We walked out of the quiet area and down the escalator to the bookshop. I saw the bookshop attendant that gave us the band-aid and asked her about the book we had just spent almost an hour looking at. She knew exactly which book it was, because 'it cost more than half the bookshelf'. I couldn't afford it at the time but decided to buy it as soon as I had the money.

We entered the elevator up to the street and, out of nowhere, I heard myself saying, "Greatness travels quietly."

Saga's face lit up as she looked up at me and said: "Mom, you think that man's pet's name was Greatness? Yes, it was. I think it was." After that, for a month or so, she would say things like "Mom, remember when Greatness was waiting for the man? Greatness is such a cute pet! Isn't she, Mom?" or "That city Greatness travelled to was magical, wasn't it?" She had taken those three words and made them her own.

Maybe that was what our grandmother was saying. With no words interfering, no descriptions and explanations given, all realities become possible at once.

15

Situations demanding metaphors involving empty jars, echoing rooms and whatnots, seemed to frequent our lives more and more. There was no silence anywhere to be found. Even the mountains were becoming noisy and busy with distant relatives making all sorts of unbearable chatter and clutter in the nature preserve where Grandma's house was still standing empty. Some were greedy and some were just curious. Mom tried her best to be patient with them all, but I wasn't always sure that being patient was a good thing. Maybe her patience was simply misguided tolerance for things that shouldn't be tolerated.

Eunice and Ivanka weren't around much. They visited occasionally, mostly to gloat at Mom's inability to handle the household without Dad's help and salary. The money Dad made in Libya was supposed to come in 'big chunks' (whatever that meant) through the government somehow, but that hadn't happened yet. Dad was due to come home soon so we weren't sure what was going on. Maybe Dad felt that it wasn't safe to send it. Maybe our father's money was held by his communist leader, or whoever was sitting behind the desk in that 'Control Centre'-marked barracks we saw in the photos. The government was taking more than two thirds of his salary so it had to be processed there, or somewhere else 'central'. That was what happened with our money when we were paid to work in the canned-food factories. We were given 3–4 levas a week now that we weren't small kids anymore. The rest of it, however little or much it was, went somewhere else. I was getting up at four o'clock in the morning and somebody else was taking the money. Was Dad getting up at four o'clock too?

Our aunt would ring the doorbell in the middle of the afternoon, just as Mom was drinking coffee with her neighbours. Mom would often have a friend or a neighbour over after morning shifts to 'talk the day out'. Eunice followed Mom's schedule somehow, so she knew how to time her visits for maximum impact. It would always seem quite innocent and friendly at the start. Eunice would march into the kitchen, pour herself some coffee and start chatting about current affairs or the weather. From there, the conversation would rapidly lean towards things that Eunice had that we didn't have, and after fifteen minutes or so, the world would be transformed into a manic nightmare, with all sorts of good, kind people dancing around her anxiously like mistreated dogs. She would stay for an hour or so, causing depression in every home on our floor, above and below. When she finally left, we would all breathe a sigh of relief.

Mom would dread Aunt's visits for weeks. Knowing that, Eunice would always appear randomly. After a while, Mom couldn't think of anything else. Her hair was starting to go grey and she had trouble sleeping. I even caught her rehearsing a conversation with Eunice once, sitting by herself, on our tidy little balcony. "Wherever you go, you leave a trail of destruction and a flood of tears. You upset people so much because they are kind to you. Even when you cry crocodile tears, you manage to spit out insults and demands. You say you are ready to listen to me. Listen to my words then! Do this! Take a week off from speaking. Smile at people and do not expect them to smile back at you. Live just one measly week without asking anyone for anything. Satisfy YOUR OWN needs, don't wait on others to do it for you. Imagine that you are exactly what you always say that you are – alone in the world. Be that! Be truly alone!"

Even in her anger, she was being too polite. It was the way she was raised by our grandmother and the way we were raised by her. And with Dad missing somewhere amongst barracks in the desert, there was nobody to teach us otherwise.

Thing is, no matter how hard we try to understand or accommodate, we may never relate to some of our relatives. Especially Eunice. She is a puzzle. Not the intriguing interesting kind of a puzzle that you can't wait to gather and complete, but the question mark that remains permanently in the line of text aiming to explain the story of my family. A question mark like that is never touched as everyone involved refuses to discover what lies underneath, in fear of demons that are too ugly to look at, or even address. The way she relates to us is odd and surprising rather than mysterious, in the same way that predators may be surprising to their victims, like when an alligator lies for days in the cool mud under the scorching sun, birds and other animals surrounding it, feeling no danger or having no memory, then suddenly it opens its mouth to swallow all of them unsuspecting creatures. We had seen bullies but never the kind that can punch you in the stomach just by looking at you. It's that kind of bully that nobody wishes to be around, see, hear or interrupt. Which is why to this day, Eunice always leads the conversation.

In my poor attempts to understand, I would ask our mother questions that absolutely nobody, especially she, could answer. 'What is the right way to be?' was a common one. Our mother would sigh and resort to simplified explanations based on obviously flawed logic. "You should be kind and do your chores. The rest will sort itself out," she would say.

"But, but…Eunice is really mean and doesn't do any chores that I can see her do, but she is always getting things and cake…and coffee…that you bought with your lunch coupons that you should use to feed yourself. And you promised me bananas for the lunch coupons. Where are my bananas?" It was an impossible conversation, and still is. I may never have a good answer.

We tend to carry other people's emotional luggage, sorted and unsorted. Some heavy and some lightweight, some unpacked and some compartmentalised, some waiting to be untangled and some left untouched. Grandma Kerana always said that this is how it should be. "One has to care for people without asking for rewards. If one was in it for the reward, one wouldn't have built orphanages and tended to the lice-infested lives of others," she would say. "You carry those people and their stories around with you, even though they've left your side long ago. There is so much you become blind to when you are like this," Mom would add. "A good friend dies and her loved ones tell you some horrifying things about her, how she tortured her daughter-in-law and harassed her grandkids, making them feel worthless. Then you realise how much you didn't know…how much suffering was left unseen and unsaid. In a way, your kindness was more important than seeing the person for what they really were – dangerously flawed."

After Troj's death, I would often resonate that maybe this is what love is…accepting this blurry image born in blindness as a true representation of people and events, a kind of 'see beauty where there is none and it will appear' – philosophy.

But what happens when beauty doesn't appear?

Troj grew up so fast that winter. Maybe it was because Dad was scheduled to return to us that same summer, the summer of '84. He figured that some serious growing up was due, so that was exactly what was done. I couldn't beat him up just by sitting on him anymore. He grew taller, his hair grew longer and wilder, his facial features grew more defined, and he started voicing wardrobe demands, something I'd been doing at his expense for years.

Watching him grow like that felt rather strange. He wasn't my 'little' brother anymore but somebody tall and strong, somebody who's opinion had to matter. He was becoming the 'man in the house' just as Dad had instructed a whole year and a half before.

He had a close friend who he called 'Brother', and they would often disappear together, either in the woods or behind the house, where they built forts filled with blankets, pillows and Dad's 'not-always-okay-ideologically-speaking' books. These forts were all ongoing projects and the furnishings in them had to be brought in every afternoon and brought back home every evening. The Romani kids would otherwise take them over and beat us with sticks and stones if we tried to come anywhere close. No matter who built what. Mom was constantly screaming at him and 'Brother' to bring stuff back with them, as she was discovering more and more things were missing. Some of that missing stuff may have been my doing as I wouldn't want to be left out, but when it came to the so called 'forts', nobody knew exactly what was going on in them and even where they were. I tried to follow them once, but I lost track when a pair of soldiers grinned at me from a nearby clearing in the woods and I had to run back where I came from. It was all a bit too secretive. It was starting to become quite clear that Troj had outgrown his need for an older sister.

There was something different about him and I couldn't put my finger on it. Mom thought that it might be 'the girls', but there were no sightings of any girls that Troj might have been interested in. None. Only him and 'Brother' strolling in and out of the house like it was their own private youth centre library. Mom would smile at him, pet him on the head, rearrange his unruly blond curls and say with pride: "You are so grown up, my boy. Look at you! No girl could ever resist you."

"Girls?" he would respond with sarcasm, pointing at me. "Like this one? Look at her with her big boobs."

"Shut your mouth, Troj!" I would scream while attacking him with whatever was on the kitchen table: knife, fork, a beer bottle, cigars or the weekly ceramic ornament. Mom's smile would instantly disappear and she would walk away shaking her head. That comment hit too close to home. 'Big boobs' run in the family and there was nothing the two of us could do about that.

I wasn't sure about boys or girls. I had a bit of a crush on a boy in my art school but then kind of felt the same way about Eime that day when I saw her pregnant belly and 'where babies come out'. It was all very unclear.

16

Winter came and went, leaving small rock-frozen piles of dirty snow and the tired whiff of drunken nights behind closed doors. Windows were gradually opened wide, weathering the winter out, small cracks at first and then wider and wider until eventually out came the clotheslines filled with wet undergarments and the occasional handkerchief.

I started attending Manasi's studio more and more frequently as his attention shifted from teaching me things to getting to know me. Whatever his intentions were, and they were impossible for me to guess, he seemed genuinely interested in knowing what I was thinking. He became excited about things that wouldn't excite any man I had previously known, not Dad, Granddad, or any of my friends' dads. I would say something or do something and he would stop everything he was doing, however important it was, and respond. That was new. I couldn't imagine anyone taking interest in the disturbingly dark poems I wrote before falling asleep or the small drawings that I made sketching ideas for imaginary murals on the frigid walls of Mom's oncology clinic. They were mostly drawings of Mom saving people (obese and old people for some obscure reason) and me and Troj watching her, waving. The waving was added for the sake of communist enthusiasm. I made it look like we were saluting Mom for doing a good job at serving The People. Manasi looked at those drawings and said, "All good apart from the waving." Then he asked me if I could make the kids 'look less like communist statues' and listened to my answers with his eyes wide open. That was new too. Throughout my entire childhood, I had never managed to make an adult stop what they were doing just to respond to something I said. They would all talk to me while still doing what they were doing before, with their eyes fixed on their hands. And they weren't all as capable as Grandma Kerana was at chatting and doing chores at the same time. Dad was pretty bad at that, so was Mom. They all pretended to listen and said things that they would say anyway, no matter what I had said to begin with. We had good conversations, don't get me wrong, but they would happen in the quiet moments after the chores were done, dinner eaten and the brandy put away in the cupboard.

Those good conversations were almost never about my drawings or poems and they all happened after a fight or a loud argument between me and Troj.

Something was going on in that studio, and somehow, Rosie knew what it was and I didn't. She would smirk and shake her head every time I started dragging my feet behind after class instead of gathering my belongings and leaving like everyone else did. The more attention I received from the Master in the Plush Chair, the more she disliked it. For a while, I thought she was jealous, but that theory was easy to disprove. There was nothing to be jealous about. She had had Manasi's full attention the entire time. Her mother and the teacher were old friends and she had known him since she was a toddler.

For the longest time, I believed that I was a stupid kid. There were plenty of facts to back that theory, especially at the time when the Manasi 'incident' took place. Something was happening to me and I had no idea what it was. It was also happening independently of Troj, which was highly unusual. I'm not even sure Troj noticed anything. He was too busy playing house with Brother.

I would come home all excited from spending time in the studio, go to our shared room to take off my school uniform, look in the mirror on my half of the shared wardrobe and lose enthusiasm altogether. Then I would spend the rest of the evening sulking, not eating anything and being irritable. Troj would occasionally enter the room without knocking, get shouted at by both our parents and respond by making mocking noises at me, which inevitably resulted in a serious fight. He seemed happy, which was incredibly irritating to me. But he was more confused and unhappy than I was. I just didn't know it at the time.

The time Manasi spent 'courting' me was short, merely a month or so, but it felt long to me, because it was made up of moments in time that seemed to last forever. I made these moments last by noticing and remembering everything. It wasn't love. I didn't love him. He was a fat, bearded teacher with a wife and three sons. I just wanted to count for something or somebody, and it almost didn't matter where and how.

And then it happened. One evening, Manasi asked me to stay behind to 'see something really interesting'. He locked the door behind the last group of kids, took me in his arms, carried me up the stairs to a gloomy, draped private room, dropped me down on the worn-out mattress and lay on me with all his hundred and ten kilogrammes of flesh. It was a strange thing that happened next. I knew very little about sex so I had no idea how it felt or even what it was. It hurt for a while and then it was over. The only image that remained was that of an overweight middle-aged man leaning over and spraying something white and creamy all over my stomach and face. My insides were sore afterwards and when I came home that night, my body was covered with some strange orange-colored rash. I was also feeling tons of guilt that I couldn't explain. I had just laid there, under a hundred and ten kilogrammes of flesh, being penetrated and left covered in sperm. I hadn't really done anything but watch it happen.

After that evening, Manasi stopped paying attention to me. It left me puzzled. I had no idea why he wouldn't notice me, and I had needed him to notice me more than any time before. It made me feel smaller than an insect and it made me surprisingly dysfunctional and dull. I would spend less time working and reading and more time dragging my feet around trying to get his attention.

Feeling small and insignificant was awkward. I knew how to be insignificant in the way Grandma Kerana had taught me. What I had learned from her was that in order to feel awe of things like beauty, nature and the universe, one had to understand one's own insignificance. There were too many people in the world that 'limited themselves by thinking that they were vastly important'. People like that 'could feel no awe'. But the kind of insignificance I was feeling in that studio wasn't complemented by The Mighty Awe; it was making me weak and sad, and, worst of all, it was making me dependent. I was craving approval for things that shouldn't matter, like the tightness of my clothes, the way my hair fell on my breasts and the attention and curiosity I exhibited every day. It was, to some extent, genuine curiosity, but mostly, it wasn't. I would listen to everything that man said, without questioning any of it.

This lasted throughout all of February and March. April came and things didn't get any better. The only thing I looked forward to was my first art practice trip. Art schools in Bulgaria tended to organise lots of art practice trips, usually in the middle of spring before tourist season or the end of summer just after the wave of Eastern European tourists at the Black Sea coast ebbed out.

That year, my school decided to send us on a mountain trip, to a city called Perushtitsa. The city was historically significant in many ways, mainly because of the Bulgarian Uprising just before the Russo-Ottoman war that ended with the liberation of Bulgaria in 1878. Five thousand out of the seven thousand villagers of a nearby city of Batak were murdered mercilessly. Perushtitsa was another city where the majority of the population was massacred because of their participation in the rebellion. Every building in that city bore traces of the massacre. We could see bullet holes and jatagan knife cuts in building facades and tree trunks. Jatagan knives were scary. They were big, sharp, shaped as an open circle and carefully crafted to cut off the head of a person just at the right angle. I had no desire to look at them, but unfortunately, they became one of the drawing exercises.

The second day of the trip felt strange from early morning. It rained though the sun was shining, and breakfast was served so early that I missed it. When we went to do our drawing exercises, I tried to stay close to my classmates but got separated and ended up sitting on a hilltop alone drawing a sheep that wasn't even there, mostly doing thick black rings on a wrinkled piece of paper. It looked horrendous and somewhat creepy, like a psychotic daydream.

Not long after I destroyed my last sheet of paper, a teacher appeared out of nowhere and told me to gather my things and follow him down. I didn't ask why, because I couldn't remember doing anything wrong and figured I better shut up and do as he says.

On the way down, we met a neighbour of ours. For some reason, he had been sent to fetch me. The teacher nodded and pointed to the neighbour adding, "It's a family thing." I picked up my bag, followed the neighbour to the car and started bombarding him with questions. He was very uncomfortable talking to me. Looking at him, I realised I had never before had a full conversation with this person. Some of my friends were his children and nephews, but I knew nothing about him at all.

The only information I could get out of him during the one-hour long trip back to Plovdiv was that my brother had 'broken his leg badly'. It sounded strange, but I didn't question it. I just chatted gladly in desperate attempts to kill the awkwardness.

When we climbed the last stairs to our flat, now even more uncomfortably quiet, he pointed to the door and disappeared as quickly as he could. I didn't have time to think about that as the door opened and a whole crowd of relatives poured out. I was led towards the kitchen without a word as everyone was hugging and grabbing me. My mother was sitting on a chair, dressed in black and surrounded by relatives. Her face and the top of her blouse were soaked in tears, but she wasn't crying, just sitting in the middle of the room making dull sounds, like an animal who had just been hit in the head with a hummer. I grabbed her feet and asked if Troj had survived his leg injury. Nobody understood what I was saying so I asked, "Is Troj alive?"

"He is dead," people answered. I couldn't figure out what to do and I couldn't ask any questions because everyone but my mother was annoyingly hysterical. So I ran out of the room and towards the end of the flat, where I had two options: the room I shared with Troj or my parents' bedroom. The latter was the obvious choice. I threw myself on our parents' bed and locked the door. My head was spinning so I grabbed it with both hands to make it stop spinning and dropped it on a pillow. My brain was showered by vivid memories almost immediately, my body felt Troj's exactly where the pillow was and I missed him the same way I would miss a leg, an arm or an eye. It was a bodily experience more than emotional. The grief didn't kick in until I saw him lying in his coffin.

My older cousins thought that I was going to kill myself too so they broke the door down. I smiled at them and told them to leave me alone. I was 'calm and collected' I said. They didn't believe me. I was telling the truth though. At that point, I was only missing an arm.

17

It was April 11th. Troj was dead, lying on a cold iron table somewhere since the day before. How come I was the last person to arrive? How come everyone else was there but me? I had spent half of this day on a stupid hill trying to draw a sheep that didn't exist on a stupid wrinkled sheet of paper, and I was angry.

What I didn't know was that April 10th was spent cleaning Troj's brain matter from the wallpaper in the living room, washing and replacing furniture upholstery with whatever wasn't drenched in blood and broken by pieces of metal. It didn't even occur to me that our living room was redecorated in just one night, that my uncles and cousins had all travelled for most of the day just to wash blood and fix whatever was fixable so that I would not see IT. IT was Death and pieces of Troj everywhere in the living room: on the windows, wallpaper, furniture, books, picture frames, photos, toys, clothes, the TV, Dad's special table and his Flora & Fauna books…on everything. I didn't see any of IT. I was spared something that damaged everyone around me for life, kept them awake for months and probably killed some, pushing them to an edge that nobody knew existed before April 10th, 1984. I am now slowly realising that I never showed any gratitude for being spared IT. I was fifteen years old; my insides were still sore from whatever happened in Manasi's studio, the rash was still itchy and I was missing a body part that was somehow shot off and spread on a cold iron table somewhere in the basement of Mom's hospital. It was just too much to handle so I didn't handle it, didn't think of it and didn't talk about it. And if you don't handle, think and talk, you can't show gratitude.

I am almost tempted to say that everything from that point on was a blur, but that would be a lie. When I was sitting alone on that hill drawing a sheep that didn't exist, I was feeling puzzled on account of my dulled near photographic memory. I couldn't understand why it didn't work. It had served me so well previously, but somehow, it had stopped working that semester. I had counted on it functioning so I was failing one exam after another and there was no explanation for it. Nobody really knew that I had it anyway so I couldn't just walk up to Mom and ask her why my ability to 'photograph' things with my eyes and then evoke the images whenever I wanted to had suddenly disappeared.

Well…guess what was back on April 11th to hit me in the front lobe like a meteor shower! Yes. That.

From that point on, everything was automatically recorded without me asking for it. I had trained my brain to not store everything by choosing where to look and for how long. Usually, I would just glance at the things I didn't want to remember and they would fade quickly. That skill was somehow lost now. I can tell you exactly what objects were placed where in the flat, what my aunts were wearing and which buttons were torn and replaced with a safety pin. I can also tell you the number of trees surrounding the funeral home and the number of flower vendors that were sitting on milk bottle trays outside the graveyard entrance. I couldn't tell you much about what things looked like during the two weeks before the funeral because I kept my eyes closed as often as I could.

I would only look when I was eating or doing a chore, but even then I would try really hard to make my brain go blank. I would focus my eyes on things that seemed neutral to me, such as a fork, a salt shaker, buttons with thread and needles stuck to them and the occasional marking pen. Everything else seemed loaded with desperation, sadness, anger and all those feelings in-between that don't really have any names.

Only a few days after the 11th, Dad came home. He wasn't supposed to come home before the summer, but there he was, all sunburned and dressed in a freshly pressed white shirt with rolled-up sleeves. He had a lot of luggage, all bursting at the seams, but he left it in the hallway unopened. I didn't think about it much at the time, but later on, it occurred to me that at least one third of it must have been shoes, tees, shorts and sweatshirts for his son to wear at football practice. Maybe even freshly printed Western magazines with all the football stars Troj admired so. I bet they were given away to neighbourhood kids. All my cousins were older, bigger or too chubby to be playing any sports.

It took two weeks for the authorities to release Troj's body so that we could bury him. Just before the funeral, local police came around asking questions that didn't make any sense to me. Why were they asking about the friend that Troj called Brother? Why did their friendship matter to them? They were just two boys playing. Why didn't they release the note that Troj left, or at least told me what was in it? Who was the man they kept referring to? Troj was seen running away from a man's house crying a month or so before April 10th. Later on, the man went to the police and told them Troj had stolen his watch. Why would Troj need his old shitty watch? There were five of them in the kitchen drawer just sitting there for him and Dad to dismantle together.

Also, a week or so before the funeral, they came and arrested Dad. They only held him for a short period of time though. It had something to do with the old hunting rifle that was found near Troj's body. The police claimed it was illegal, but it wasn't. It was a gift to Grandpa Troj from all his partisan friends that survived the fascist occupation. It had a certificate and everything.

There was too much happening that I didn't know anything about and it put me in a state of numbness. I didn't really know how to talk to any of the people around me. I just went with the waves as they hit the shore. I let them carry me around like a loose anchor. There was a lot of guilt involved as I felt absolutely useless. There must have been something for me to do as the only child remaining, some universal chore that would just make things better. But there wasn't. Grandma Kerana used to say that we 'must rise above the sway of things', which I didn't do. Going with the sway wasn't even an option because this wasn't a sway but ten hurricanes that hit at once without a warning or time given to recuperate. I had no idea how to make myself useful, or at least not useless.

The funeral date was set as soon as Troj's body was released. I don't remember being told about it. Nobody said a word. I was just told to dress nicely, and we were driven to a funeral home near the graveyard. I'm guessing that they kept me on a tight leash because I was acting weirdly. I would chat away and smile, like nothing had happened but often with my eyes closed. I didn't feel close to any of my relatives so I couldn't really tell them that my eyes were closed because my memory was being unnecessarily overactive. They would have thought that I'd lost my mind completely or was escaping reality by inventing some ridiculous superpowers that I didn't actually have.

Every single one of our relatives was dressed in black so I knew that the funeral was happening later on. I kept my head down and my eyes closed as much as I could. Looking in the mirror was not an option so I have no recollection of my clothes other than the dark-blue shimmer of the buttons and my cream-colored bra showing. Our mirror was in the wardrobe in the room that Troj and I shared. It was next to Troj's neatly folded clothes and his lavender towel that Mom always kept fluffy and clean. Opening that wardrobe door was unthinkable.

As we pulled up to the graveyard parking lot, more people appeared. Eunice and Grandma Ivanka must have been somewhere, but for the first time since I became self-aware, the two of them didn't matter. They didn't even exist that day, if you ask me.

There must have been hundreds more attending, but not all of them were friends or relatives. Some were drawn by the mere news value of Troj's violent and mysterious death and the opportunity to tell people that they attended the funeral of 'that boy'. They were not let in. I heard my oldest uncle's voice in the crowd: "This is for family only, people. Have some respect, please!" Then I heard disappointed mumbling and my mother's hiccups, and we started walking towards the door.

There must have been a sermon of some kind, but I wasn't there to see it. I ran back out as fast as I could. How could I ever explain that one look was enough for my overactive brain to forever record everything? The coffin was of dark mahogany-colored wood. It had a purple velvet label encased in a bronze frame just above Troj's head. If you imagine a specimen in a lab being prepared for a natural history exhibit, like a taxidermy bird or a squirrel on a tree branch, you would know exactly what I was looking at. There was a neat bandage around Troj's head, held together with a safety pin tucked underneath the neck. There was makeup applied to his skin, but I could still see the small birthmark underneath his ear. I had the same one. His fingernails were cleaner than usual and he was dressed in a football jersey. So that's where Dad's gifts went. Somebody finally opened the big suitcase.

There was no way I could possibly stay in that room and feel the trembling of the crowd as it was pressing against the coffin, like my body was the only thing stopping them from piling up on top of it. There was no way for me to know if it would have been easier to understand this coffin and the body inside it if we were alone, just the three of us, three confused bodies that were missing their limbs. There is a slight possibility that we would have joined our three bodies, holding arms and heads together to make a stronger one, just for the time being, until we could stand on our remaining limbs. If we were left alone. But we weren't left alone. For some reason, I was kept far away from my mother. Relatives would come in-between and stop my every attempt to touch her or hold her. Like they were claiming her for themselves, like they used to do before I was born and before my father came along on his Vespa, threw his cigarette to the ground, grabbed her by her waist and drove away.

The same thing happened when we entered the funeral home. Some friends and relatives were already waiting in the huge cold marble-clad hall, surrounding the coffin, leaving only three carefully calculated spots for us: one for Mom above Troj's head, one for Dad slightly to the side and one for me on Troj's left side. I have no idea why they did that, but it was an intrusion and I felt it so strongly that my whole body rejected it. I scratched and punched my way out of the crowd and ran back outside right in the arms of the first person that was roughly my age.

There was a collusion of some kind and the impact of it was the strongest thing I've ever felt. It was much stronger than having a seizure, giving birth or being frightened to death. There was a reality colliding inside another one and it came as a hit to the head that lasted for a really long time. I choked, fell backwards and then started sobbing uncontrollably. If there was a higher power somewhere in the universe, I knew exactly what it was doing at that moment in my timeline. All the parallel universes where Troj was present after April 10th, 1984, collapsed simultaneously and this higher power was letting me know.

The physical separation between the three of us continued until relatives and friends left the flat. After that, there was silence and lots of it. It was almost like we needed to learn how to talk to each other again. Dad being away for so long made everything even more awkward. He wasn't the same person that climbed the bus stairs clutching an overstuffed suitcase two years before. He had stopped smoking and kept a healthy diet, not to better his appearance but as a way to cope with the hellish working conditions that he endured in Africa. He not only looked different but his manners had softened, and he was a lot quieter. Losing his only son must have done some real damage, but he never talked about it. His heart just broke, and it broke in silence because Mom somehow claimed all available grief just as she always claimed us children, like she was the only parent. Dad and I were left to deal with our own feelings quietly and in separate rooms.

We tried our best to not blame Mom for hogging the spotlight on grief; it was her way of letting us know that she felt responsible for what had happened. But she was entitled to that spotlight not only because she was the one left in charge of the home and children and failed but because she was the one who found him. The sight of her child in pieces in the middle of a room full of blood is an image of unimaginable pain. Dad and I were known for our vivid imaginations so we could see the scene in our heads, but we didn't suffer that first initial blow to the head of universes collapsing and realities of death and absolute endings being born out of what used to be love and joy. I wouldn't have survived a blow like that. Neither would Dad. To some extent, we had time to grasp it all before we could imagine the scene, piecing it bit by bit rather than living through its absolute impact. We were lucky. And so we welcomed Mom to the stage and bowed to her sorrow.

A week or so after the funeral, I went back to school. In a way, I was grateful for having some time off from committing to somebody else's grief, even if it was my mother's. My body felt a new kind of numbness, like it wasn't mine. I was walking around, sitting down, eating, looking and listening, but whatever body was around that mind of mine didn't really belong to me, it was lent to me for temporary usage, to support my overactive brain and assist it until the actual body of Iva returned to take its rightful place.

School was strange for a couple of months. It was quite clear that all 120 or so students knew about Troj and his alleged suicide. It was an ugly scary word that nobody would hint, let alone say. Rosie was the only one who said anything of substance about the way she felt thinking of me and Troj, and the strange thing was that for the first time since I got to know her, I didn't feel connected to her. The words came a bit too easy. Although they probably weren't, they did sound very much rehearsed. I watched her lips move and registered the words, but at that moment, she became a stranger. That impression somehow decided to last forever. We were friends, but I didn't feel love for her any more.

Not being in awe of Rosie was scary but oddly liberating. It was one of those things that left when Troj left. So did my sense of entitlement, my self-love and my ability to see myself in other people. From this day on, nobody else's shoes fit me. There was nobody like me out there. Those missing limbs of mine...everybody could see them now. The ugly red scars that appeared where those missing limbs used to be became the focus of attention of friend and foe alike. Even Manasi acknowledged the scars and showed surprising respect. That didn't last long though. After demanding to know if I had written new poetry or drawn new mural sketches, and hearing that I haven't, he appointed Rosie to be my keeper and spy and went back to being himself. In a matter of weeks, the hundred and ten kilos of flesh were on top of me sweating again. This time, I didn't even care.

Rosie was trying her best to be a good friend. But she didn't know what that meant in my case. I don't blame her for becoming my, by Manasi appointed, keeper. She thought I needed his attention and acknowledgement to feel better, to be able to focus on my talent again and get on with my life. I watched her try really hard and selfishly enjoyed seeing her fail. The more she tried, the less it mattered. To me, she seemed privileged and overconfident, like somebody who believed in having answers without asking questions.

One day, I caught myself pretending to listen and the whole friendship thing felt meaningless. It was the day I threw Manasi under the bus.

"I'm fucking him."

"Fucking who?"

"Manasi."

"Oh…Really?"

"Yeah, really. It's been going on for a while."

"Did you want to?"

"I don't know. It just happened."

"Shit! Shit! You know…he fucked somebody else. Do you remember that girl that was really gifted and absolutely stunning?"

"The blond one?"

"Yeah, the one whose sister was killed in Sofia."

"I haven't seen her since…spring."

"She is in and out of mental institutions."

"Because of Manasi?"

"Maybe."

We were quiet for a long while, each of us thinking separate thoughts about things we didn't know much about and were unwilling to discuss. Some things are better left unsaid or even misunderstood. Being stuck between childhood and womanhood is confusing.

I didn't visit the studio for several weeks. It just didn't occur to me to go there when things at home were so awkward and in dire need of my attention. Mom, who was a firm believer in natural remedies, went from an all-knowing wise woman to a pill-popping nervous wreck in a matter of weeks. It pained me to see her like that, but at least, she was coping. Whatever she was right now was better than the lifeless shell I saw when I didn't have my eyes closed before and just after the funeral. It wasn't a person yet, but there was some kind of life in there, some kind of rage even. That was a very good sign.

When I finally showed up at Manasi's studio, I was greeted with utter discontent. He saw me coming, rushed downstairs and blocked the entrance. Some of the children he tutored were still leaving so he just stood there, staring at me with his eyes popping like he had no eyelids, with children trying to squeeze past his belly. I had no idea what this was about so my heart started pounding uncontrollably and the adrenalin rush became nearly unbearable as I tried to stop myself from running away.

When the last child left, Manasi closed the door and walked towards me. I couldn't move. He didn't hold me or even touch me. Instead, he started whispering through his teeth and it sounded like a snake's whisper. I didn't speak snake so I started blinking in confusion, realising I couldn't understand what he was saying; he stepped away and repeated the last couple of sentences.

"You juvenile piece of...I thought you were a woman, but I was mistaken. Juvenile is what you are. Rosie told us everything."

"Who is us?"

"Who do you think? Rosie's mother and I. She is a friend you know...a really really good friend. And a woman. Not like you. Who do you think you are? And my wife...she can never know. Are you hearing me? She has more womanhood in her little finger than you have in your whole body. Threatening to out me...Outrageous!"

The truth was I blanked at that point. Whatever was happening seemed to have nothing to do with me. It was all about him, Rosie's mother and his wife who was apparently a woman, whatever that meant.

My imagination started spinning around scenarios where Rosie's mother, the opera-singing woman, dragged information out of my friend using all sorts of torture methods and tools, including thin and sharp make-up brushes, tweezers, spoons, fancy shoelaces and crystal glasses. The crazy neighbour appeared just after Rosie spilled the beans and started rubbing her swollen belly with their finest cognac. She had a big beach hat with flowers on it and a red dress. Rosie was left breathing heavily as the two women left the room dancing with maracas in their hands 'click-clack-smack-crack' and off they went.

I never saw the insides of that studio again.

I didn't really talk to my father that year. The only time we had a real conversation in 1984, apart from the necessary back and forth of everyday life, was on Christmas Day evening.

Christmas wasn't celebrated during communist times. There was a thing called Christmas behind closed doors, but Santa Claus was replaced with his imp communist twin named Father Frost. The two of them looked exactly the same and whatever Santa Claus did, his twin did too. Father Frost brought presents, climbed down chimneys and ate the porridge we left for him outside our front door.

I wasn't looking forward to Christmas 1984. I just wanted the worst year of my young life gone. My parents were spending the last week in the village with Ivanka and Eunice, which made me wish I could just sleep through the holidays. But sleep was the one thing I couldn't do, not because of what was going on in my head but because of how unbearably fake and intrusive my relatives were. Apart from my parents and my two very attractive second cousins, every other person was an overeating, gossip-spewing, insensitive excuse for a human, not to mention Eunice. She was at her absolute worst, and it was inexcusable this time because of what happened to us. Not only was she gossiping and joking about it, she was also poking at my father in careless attempts to make him see Mom as the culprit and the one who didn't protect his children and the family. I couldn't stand her. I wished her dead so much that I turned to black magic. I thought of a really good curse, wrote it down on a piece of paper, spat on it and started looking for a good spiritually significant place to hide it to maximise its powers and range.

There was an attic above the storage room in the main house. Ivanka didn't have the guts to open it because it was where Grandpa Troj stored his most precious possessions, from his fishing gear to old photos from his guerrilla days. It was the perfect place for hiding my curse so I waited until dinner was served, ate a little and sneaked out when they all started drinking.

The main house was darker than usual; the sun had already set and the broken streetlight outside the window flickered releasing annoyingly frequent sparks. Ivanka tended to recycle things that Mom didn't want in the flat so my old Communist-style jungle motif kid's curtains had somehow become centrepieces and they were more or less solid cotton.

I opened the curtains a little to let the moonlight in, carried the big living room chair to the storage room, climbed on it and opened the small dusty hatch above my head. I hid the neatly folded piece of paper under one of the boards and looked around. Everything was as I remembered it. The fishing rod was there. So were Grandpa's hunting books and his boots and the petroleum green coat that smelled of mothballs. The two cardboard boxes where he kept documents, photos and his medals were left slightly open, but I assumed it was because The Party took his medals for the funeral and didn't care enough to close the boxes properly. At that point, I noticed that something was missing. Grandpa kept at least one case of ammunition next to his hunting boots. It was a red dusty box with black unreadable lettering and a golden stamp. It wasn't there. I wondered if that was what killed Troj and looked for his fingerprints around the square space where the box used to be. It was too dark to see anything.

Father Frost came late on Christmas day. It was almost midnight when he showed up, and it wasn't pleasant. I had already gone to bed in the living room where Mom sent me after dinner. The adults gathered downstairs in the summer kitchen, and as the evening progressed, their voices became louder than a September 9th parade. I wasn't even dreaming yet so it must have been minutes after I had fallen asleep. I woke up from the noise of somebody falling over the garden furniture, and by the time I opened my eyes, Father Frost was leaning on the window next to my bed. He had no teeth and I could see his big purple tongue. His beard was fake and considerably dirtier than it should have been and one of his hands was almost entirely fingerless. I ran downstairs in my pyjamas, scared to death and screaming.

Ivanka was already outside with a stick. She took one look at her drunken nephew Genjo and dropped the stick to the ground with a heavy sigh.

This nephew of hers had become quite a nuisance lately. He was constantly drunk and not very sharp-witted to begin with. Nevertheless, people in the village considered him to be rather harmless and because of his 'jolly' appearance, he was often tasked with small jobs involving costumes. Thus, Genjo being Granit's Father Frost of Christmas 1984.

Mom wasn't amused this time. She pulled me behind her back and started yelling at Genjo. That scared him. He wasn't used to Mom yelling at him. She would usually feed him, take care of his scratches and cuts, and if she was in the mood, lecture him about the pitfalls of drinking bottle after bottle of cheap 40% liquor. The sight of her actually yelling at him made him shiver and he looked genuinely frightened. At some point, it became clear to him that he was yelled at because of me so he stretched his arm to clap me on the head. Dad appeared out of nowhere and punched him.

I had never seen my Dad punch anybody. Troj and I had endured the occasional beating, but being slapped by Mom was somehow much worse so we considered Dad's punches more of a necessary argument-stopper. This wasn't a slap. Genjo fell to the ground like a locomotive hit him. I could almost see the wind created by Dad's fist hitting him just after the main punch in the neck. It was like Thor's infamous hammer.

I didn't know how to react to that. It made me laugh but only on the inside. I had to make sure that Genjo wasn't dead though; Dad had already been arrested once that year because of Grandpa's rifle. He didn't need more trouble in his life, especially from that no-good cousin of his. Genjo was alive, but my Dad's punch had definitely put him to sleep. I knew that because I poked him with my foot, which wasn't a great idea since I wasn't wearing any shoes in the middle of winter, and I felt the wrath of both Mom and Ivanka at the same time. Thankfully, Eunice was too drunk to join in.

I couldn't sleep after the commotion so I put some clothes on and decided to hang around the adults in the summer kitchen. That wasn't really how things were done in the family, but they made an exception this time. By two o'clock, everybody but Dad and I had fallen asleep somewhere.

One of my father's superpowers in younger years was the ability to hold his alcohol. I have seen him replace glasses of water with pints of liquor and drink them as if they were just soda, but I have never in my life seen him drunk. The only thing that happened after drinking too much alcohol was that he became a slower, mellower talker. The soft tone of his voice and the slow pace of his thoughts made our conversation surprisingly easy and pleasant that evening.

"Sorry about that idiot outside, Iva! He is such a nuisance that man."
"It's not your fault, Dad. It kind of is your fault that he is sleeping it off on the pavement though."

My father smiled and nodded, looking at his glass somewhat lost in his thoughts.

"It's my pleasure, darling girl. My absolute pleasure. He did scare you."
"He just startled me is all; I'm not so easily scared."

Dad smiled and nodded again, then looked at me somewhat puzzled.

"Why were you sleeping upstairs? Did your mother tell you off or something?"

"Oh no…it's Christmas and Mom thought that you and the others would be too noisy for me to sleep."

He took a small sip of brandy from a shot glass then sat in silence looking at me.

"Are you okay?"

"Yeah, he is sleeping on the pavement, isn't he?"

"I don't mean him…Are you okay otherwise?"

"I'm okay, I just wish this dumb holiday was over already."

"I'm not okay. Africa was…different. But home is not better. Nothing makes sense around here either. Everyone is lobotomised and they don't even know it. The Arabs are clever though. Nobody over there works. The gastarbeiters do it all. Wipe their asses if they got paid to do it. It's the way it's gonna be here one day, you know, when Communism is kaput. The old communist aristocracy will be sitting on benches chewing tobacco like the Arabs, while the rest of us are wiping their asses. And you, with your talent and your pretty hair…maybe you can marry well. Who knows."

I didn't say anything, just helped my father to the bedroom and closed the door.

18

Going back to school in the beginning of 1985 was like a sudden awakening. School didn't start right away. The semester began with a school trip to Sofia, our nation's capital. Rosie and I didn't do much together anymore so the pleasure of my company could be had by anyone. My wardrobe was vastly improved by the contents of Dad's Africa suitcase and the other students showed their appreciation openly, especially a boy I liked. He invited me to walk with him to the National Art Academy when we arrived in Sofia. His big brother studied there and he wanted to show me around.

He had the same birthday as I did, July 1st, so I started calling him July. That afternoon, I spent walking the streets of Sofia talking to July about art and theatre and being painfully shy about my knowledge of the arts and current events. Walking in silence and using awkward body language to convey thoughts or feelings was not something I did often. I must have really liked the boy. And when we arrived at the National Art Academy, the fear and shyness took over completely. It didn't help that his brother's work was impressive, so much so that he was already winning European awards, which made him somewhat of a celebrity.

They were very much alike. Both had round glasses, just like John Lennon's, and unruly brown hair, cut short at the neck but left long at the front, so they both kept blowing at their foreheads in sometimes synchronised attempts to move their forelocks to the side. It made my heart beat really fast, but it didn't help my shyness. Most thoughts that crossed my mind didn't make it out of my mouth, but that was perfectly fine as the more I smiled and nodded, the more I seemed to charm them both. They appeared rather motivated to teach me things and take care of me. It was almost like July was lending me his big brother for an afternoon just so that I wouldn't miss Troj too much.

My allowance for the rest of the month was spent on coffee and art materials, and by the time we all boarded the train back to Plovdiv, I was completely broke, so broke that I couldn't even afford a cup of tea in the train cafeteria. It didn't really matter. My head was full of happy thoughts, and I wanted everybody to know so I stuck my head out of the nearest window and started shouting at the top of my lungs. The cold wind was beating my face and messing with my afro hair, but I didn't care one bit.

That night, I developed a nasty ear infection, and Dad had to drive me to the hospital.

There was blood and some other colorless fluid coming out of my ears. The left ear was far worse than the right. It hurt so much that I pushed my head through the metal bars of my bed frame. It helped a little.

Mom was working her last nightshift for the week so she rushed down to the parking lot just as Dad and I arrived. She took us to an old yellow building with a leaky roof and broken windows. That made me cry out, but I somehow managed to muffle the cry in the knitted scarf gently wrapped around my neck and ears by my very scared father. We walked through a long corridor and just as we started bending away from the low ceilings, we came to an intersection that led us to a nicer, more hospital-like wing. Mom was wearing her white coat so the nurse nodded and waved to the hospital staff to take me in saying: "One of our kids needs help." I don't know exactly what they did, but they worked fast and the bleeding and pain stopped.

I had to stay for ten days so my guess was they probably punctured an eardrum or two and had to make sure that my head didn't get infected. July came to see me on the third day and it made me insanely happy. He was very polite and kept smiling apprehensively. He brought some flowers and chocolates so we ate and smiled at each other. It's probably not true, but I can swear remembering how utterly dumb and awkward I was, smiling like an imbecile and stuffing my mouth with chocolates without saying a word.

I'm not sure why I needed to stay in that broken down hospital for so long. I didn't do much more than lie around in a teddy bear-adorned nightgown drawing and reading incomprehensible books about Chinese philosophy and Egyptian art. It was quite clear my mother had an agreement with the hospital staff to keep me there until I was completely out of danger. Despite the bed shortage, everyone seemed to honour the agreement without as much as a mention. It wasn't up for discussion and the whole town was in on it.

Being away from art school for two whole weeks burdened me with the immense task of catching up on classes taught on the fly and without any notes and records. I somehow thought that the drawings I did in my hospital bed would buy me some time and a little acknowledgment. Clearly, I had chosen quantity before quality because the day I walked into the classroom with my thick bundle of sketches was the day I heard the sound of fifty people gasping in disappointment for the first time. The teacher's hostile attitude and somewhat misogynist sense of humour didn't make it easier for me as the class shifted from disappointment to loud mockery and laughter.

What confused me the most was the fact that I really liked my drawings. The model was a girl that I had befriended in the hospital. She had the bed next to mine for about half a day but was moved to another room after Mom's daily visit. Although we only spent four measly hours together, I completely and utterly missed her so I walked up and down the corridor until I found her. She seemed tired from either her condition or her treatment so I brought her some tea from the 'luxurious' and off-limits staff cafeteria.

Her slender figure and somewhat cat-like movements inspired much curiosity during my hospital stay. I didn't even think of July that week. She was keeping me busy laughing and drawing. She would walk around the room squatting and making silly noises while encouraging me to sketch. I made about sixty drawings on large sheets of grey paper. The charcoal drawings were really nice, especially the ones of her squatting in her pyjamas. Strangely enough, the teacher picked exactly those drawings to ridicule. He smiled sarcastically and asked if the figure was 'masturbating' or showing me how to 'perform cunnalingus on myself'. The class exploded with laughter, and my heart started beating at a life-threatening pace, or at least that's what it felt like.

I never saw that girl again, but undoubtedly, there is a thick bundle of proof of her cat-like existence somewhere in a drawer in my parents' storage room.

It is not entirely clear why and who decided to keep so much of my early 'artwork' despite my loud protests. It could be Dad, but that was very unlikely. Mom is the true hoarder in our family. She collects useless trinkets like it's some kind of lovely valuable memorabilia. Oddly enough, Troj's things were still kept on display after the funeral. Even small things that he played with or just touched at some point during his thirteen-years-short life were put on shelves rather than hidden in drawers. That was some divergent behavior on our mother's part. My entire life was spent knowing that Mom enjoyed putting things in boxes and drawers more than she enjoyed the actual things. This was very unusual, and it lasted for a whole year, until my sister was born.

My sister came out of nowhere. Mom had always said that she couldn't have any more children. Both Troj and I were caesarean babies and the mere fact that we were born healthy was a well-known and often discussed miracle.

Mom looked pregnant for two to three months, starting just around the 10th of April, 1985, and right in the middle of June came my sister – a chubby baby with big eyes and straight black hair. Mom was genuinely happy, and for the first time in my life, she was unafraid to show it. The baby made her laugh, smile and cry all at the same time, and it was wonderful and a little bit scary to watch her jump from one extreme emotion to another, but no woman deserved a sea of uncontrollable happy emotions more than she did.

My sister was given the name Darina. Darina has its roots in the old Bulgarian word 'dar', meaning 'valuable gift', which made sense I suppose, but since I was only sixteen years old, it wasn't up to me. If anyone cared to ask or know, I would have advised the choice of a name that wasn't a clear reminder of what her arrival in this world did for Mom's grief. Nobody asked.

Dad's view on the matter of having a baby so soon after Troj's death was never to be revealed to us other mortals. Whatever was going through his mind was forever sealed inside his post-Africa reserved demeanour. Somewhere between not being consulted and being resented for withdrawing into his hobbies, my father decided to live his life outside home. And so did I.

None of that was the baby's fault. She was full of life and her commitment to loving unconditionally was unrivalled. She was a gift all right, a sweet person in the making that never quit smiling. I can't, for the life of me, remember her crying, not before she hit puberty anyway. Our lives were so much better with Dari in them, no matter how poor we felt or how stressed we were.

She grew bigger with every hour it seemed. In a matter of months, she had brand new tiny teeth and started crawling. And a couple of months later, she started walking in that wobbly manner that only chubby toddlers and drunk Father Frosts can master. Every step she took on her small round feet was a step of enjoyment and appetite for life. I loved having her around, playing with her and feeding her. Putting her to bed and reading stories was my favourite thing to do, although she smiled at everything, even at heroes dying.

Mom was having the time of her life with the baby, but after a while, she started missing her patients. All through 1985 and 1986, patients and colleagues would visit, not only to see her and the baby but to keep her informed about new equipment, new staff and new procedures. Cancer-free women and men brought her gifts and expensive cakes. As a private person, she was permitted to receive gifts and her grateful patients didn't disappoint. Sometimes they brought children and relatives with them so they too could express their gratitude. Occasionally, the mothers of children who died of cancer in Mom's care would show up at the door, full of grief and hoping for answers. Mom didn't disappoint either. She received them calmly but openly and let them cry on her shoulder while offering not only her embrace but words of wisdom. Most of those words were Grandma Kerana's, but nobody else but I knew that. Increasingly uncomfortable amidst the ever-lasting embraces and crying of adults, I spent less time with my mother and more time playing with Dari. Mom didn't like that one bit, but who was she to blame me? My Troj-shaped limbs were still missing and I was very confused about a lot of things…art, love, gender, sexuality, school, mothers, the future and all its possible scenarios, but most of all, I was confused about the sheer amount of attention adults always demanded of me, from the day I was born and throughout my life, in every waking moment. It was obvious that Mom mistook this for lack of empathy. But how much empathy for strangers could a child possibly muster when all that mattered was everybody else's needs?

Mom went back to work eventually. I was more than happy to become a surrogate mother once again so I welcomed all the dusty chores that everyday life in our Tracia flat had to offer. But this time, it felt like a job and, contrary to previous commitments to siblings and parents, I didn't do this one for Mom, I did it for Dad and Dari.

Dad seeing me happy seemed somehow important. Whenever he was in the flat at the same time as Mom, he was told to do things or take responsibility for things undone or forgotten. I felt sorry for him, although 'sorry' doesn't even begin to describe the myriad of feelings that washed over me when Dad was there. It was a concoction of sadness, guilt, shame, pain, love, anxiety and a multitude of other emotions with no names. Mostly, I was afraid that we might lose Dad too. I knew very little about married life, but somehow, I was aware of the pitfalls of living in your head because your partner won't budge an inch out of her comfort zone. It wasn't even about Mom or whatever shortcomings came along with tragedy. It was all about the impossibility of shared life on account of the unbearable pain felt whenever one exited the cosy comforts of denial. We were all very much aware that there was nothing we could do but let life take its course, even if it meant giving up and living outside of the family.

That denial of Mom's was a strange and ever-growing beast. She was constantly smiling when sadness was due and tears were swallowed momentarily whenever her emotions prevailed. Keeping a happy face became her number one job, all at the expense of common sense and honesty. Dad started spending more and more time outside the house, and Mom's work became once again the dominant topic of conversation in the home. For the longest time, I thought that these changes only concerned us and were visible to Dad and me alone. But I was mistaken. Eunice saw it too.

She showed up on our doorstep one day bearing gifts. Mom wouldn't willingly let her in, but she had promised Dad in an argument that lasted for a whole week. We didn't want Eunice anywhere near the baby, and Mom was literally allergic to her, but promises were always kept in our family.

Mom started twitching and rushed into the kitchen to make coffee. She took out the coffee beans first but immediately changed her mind and reached for a jar of precious instant coffee. No price could be put on getting Eunice out of the flat as quickly as humanly possible. I have never in my life seen anyone prepare a cup of coffee so quickly. It was like watching a robot from a sci-fi film, automotive and moving at the speed of light.

From the very moment Eunice's lips parted, peace left the building. We didn't know how to talk to her in anger so we just let her talk hoping that our ability to block words from entering our ears was somehow still strong. But our blocking efforts were less than adequate that day. Whenever she saw us looking away or noticed our disregard for her words, she paused and uttered something shocking or highly insensitive. I managed to let some of it bounce off me, but after a while, she regrouped and said, "Hopefully, this one will not be deviant and disgusting," pointing to my baby sister. At this point, Mom excused herself, walked to the bedroom and closed the door. Eunice didn't even turn around. She reached for a napkin, put three slices of Mom's freshly baked marble cake in it and dropped it in her big brown leather bag. She then looked around for more things to take, but I had already secured the instant coffee by jumping on top of it and grabbing the jar with both hands so she smirked and left the flat.

Mom and I said nothing all day. It was clear that we wanted to. Our eyes met and our lips parted to speak out words more than once, but we just couldn't.

However sad or angry Eunice made us, we somehow always regrouped quickly and went back to ignoring her existence in our lives. But this time was different. Judging from Mom's behavior, Eunice's last words bore some kind of specific meaning that was entirely lost on me. My baby sister was absolutely adorable so calling her deviant and disgusting was cruel but laughably absurd, so the question was why Eunice's words caused such upset. Was she aiming at somebody else? Was it me? It couldn't be, because I couldn't think of anything I might have done to deserve such slander. Was she talking about my parents? She wouldn't have the guts to talk this way about Mom to her face and Dad had never given her a reason to be mean. Was she talking about Troj? That would definitely do it. But why? What was so disgusting about a boy that wasn't even there anymore?

My aunt and the likes of her were always confusing to me. She seemed so normal, well-functioning and sometimes even well-educated. It was bewildering how quick she moved from spewing horrible comments about a 'feminine' man she met on the street to giving sound medical advice that might actually help somebody. She was such a contradiction to the idea of a decent human being that the only way I could handle her existence was to imagine her as a character in a story. In my imaginary world, fictional adults were allowed to be dubious because they all got punished at the end. Once she was a goat with a horse's head that was slaughtered. The goat's stubby short-legged body seemed to be an appropriate allegory for her clumsy manners and often loud and aggressive behavior, while the horse's head clearly represented some level of education and understanding of the world. There was nothing wrong with the two parts, the body and the head, on their own, but the many different combinations I explored, however thoughtful, seemed either hilarious or grotesque and sometimes plain ugly, so at the end of the day, when I killed the beast, it felt pleasurable. But it was a double-edged pleasure. On one side, I felt drawn to this strange character that was somehow related to me because she was the only woman I knew who didn't stay quiet while the men were talking…naha, she ate men for breakfast and that was impressive to me. That said, the pleasure I felt from watching her climb over the men was quickly pushed aside by my confusion over her hatred of all creatures she deemed 'deviant'. I sat there confused, day after day, scratching my young head and wondering how many of us were like the goat-horses I drew, soaking up bits of information from whatever surrounded us, chopping it up and turning it into prejudice, possible advantages against others, and mostly garbage that we one day may cast upon a small child obliterating its hope of ever becoming somebody with a meaning and purpose. I didn't automatically see myself as a goat-horse or another of my dubious creatures, but

I often stood surrounded by them thinking that I sooner or later will have to become one with this world of distorted creatures that never looked outside their windows and saw beauty.

19

Having a baby sister at the age of sixteen had its perks. I was more than happy to be the talk of the school for something other than the mysterious and violent death of a sibling. I took Dari to every school event that allowed outsiders, and she embraced it with the unbridled excitement that only a toddler could muster. She made everyone happy, students and teachers alike. Unfortunately, my own happiness was ever declining, no matter what Dari did. And she really tried.

The main thing that clouded my happy days was that July avoided me. Every morning, before a class, I browsed the crowds at the school entrance looking for him, my heart beating faster and faster as his usual band of boys appeared. But every time our eyes met, he looked down at his feet and hurried away leaving me hanging with a frozen smile on my lips. This was happening again and again for a month or so until one day a piece of paper with my poem on it flew right at me on the schoolyard. The piece of paper was tossed from one person to another until it hit somebody clumsy and flew in my face.

To a layman, or somebody who didn't know that this poem was written by a teenage girl, the writings in question would have seemed fairly innocent. They could have been the fruit of an absent-minded artist drinking summer wine, or the delirious creations of a feverish poet whose days were numbered. But in that schoolyard, everybody knew everything, and it quickly became clear that there was something seriously wrong with me.

The poem was not about July or my personal tragedies, it was about Manasi. And although there were no names given, it was obvious that at least one person in the poem was an older man and he wasn't having an innocent encounter with the young poet, so to speak.

When I wrote this particular poem, I thought it to be a true masterpiece – a categorisation that faded with time. The so-called poem started with a vague description of a room full of books and etchings, then moved to our faces and the smell of beard in the wind, at which point it made a twisted dark turn towards a testament of 'naked loyalty' and thundered to its abrupt end by numbering things that mattered in the context: pubic hair, orange-colored rash above my left thigh, lips left unkissed despite plenty of violence, and the amount of penis versus young vagina in-and-outs registered that day. I was counting apparently.

No wonder July avoided me, whatever was below my waist was forever discarded. It wasn't even a thing of substance anymore like…bones, skin or flesh, just grey mass that no one wanted to see or touch.

That summer, I didn't come home until I had done 'the Jack Kerouac thing'. I knew that my parents would never let me go on the road so I pretended to go on a prolonged summer work camp and headed to the Black Sea accompanied by my newly found and unexpectedly physically strong friend Dora.

Summer work camp was not an uncommon thing in Eastern Europe. It was basically a slightly fancier word for cheap child labour. It was obligatory unless one could provide a doctor's note and even then it was difficult to prove that one was 'unfit to serve'. My mother was usually quick to dismiss my pleas for a doctor's note. She could possibly provide one, but a part of her was fine with child labour given all her siblings and herself spent most summers working on other people's fields. Besides, she was 'very busy with the baby'.

I hated summer work camp with passion, but that year, I was planning a sweet escape so working in the Asenovgrad can factory was not as bad. I spent most of the time doing a lousy job peeling tomatoes. We whispered 'Let the Germans eat our crappy peels' to each other and giggled while keeping an eye on the guard.

After the obligatory four weeks, Dora came to pick me up from Asenovgrad and explained her plan to me. She wanted the full Jack Kerouac experience so I was brainwashed to only take one small duffel bag with me. My copy of Jack Kerouac's *On the Road* was in it as well as some underwear, a pair of light-blue trousers (my Africa gift from Dad), one more black top and a jacket. The plan was to take a bus to the Black Sea and sleep at our art school summer camp for a night and then continue down the coast. July's class were already doing their biannual art practice there so getting smuggled into camp sounded like a good idea.

Well…the bus ride didn't happen. We went to the bus station and queued for about fifteen minutes. I was so excited about our trip that I just wouldn't stop talking about it. "Oh, this is going to be soooo much fun! I'm loving your jeans skirt by the way. Have you seen mine? I made it myself out of my old jeans and a blue bag I found in the closet. It's a little short, but it looks good. Don't you think? Shall we sit on the front or in the back? The back is cooler, I think, it's like we own the fucking bus. Don't you think?" And so on until Dora started crying.

It wasn't my incessant chatter that caused her to start crying, although I thought so for a moment. When it was our turn to buy bus tickets, she discovered that more than half of our money was gone. She was trying to explain something to me, but I could barely understand her. She was almost choking with tears and the only thing that made it out of her mouth was: "He took...everything...it was mine...father...drunk bastard...I hate...hate...hate...bald ass...with the f-f-f-fuck-in' belt...stink of fish...I won't...no matter what...he...does...hick...to me..."

I didn't ask.

That same evening, we almost joined the 'truck-girls'. They were mostly young Romani kids, some as young as 12, selling blow jobs to whomever drove by. Some left with the truckers and were never seen again.

We didn't want to get raped so we found a small crossroad off the main freeway that was about three hundred yards from the truckers' usual hangout and started waving our thumbs. We were soon picked up by a trucker, but Dora knew the man so we jumped in the back and laughed the whole four hours to the town of Primorsko, relieved that we weren't in any immediate danger. The man was a former neighbour of Dora's so they spent a lot of time chatting about his kids and the other people they both knew from the 'old neighbourhood'. Strangely enough, we were never asked why we were hitchhiking instead of taking the train like normal people. The man was quite reserved and kept looking at Dora in a funny way, like he knew something about her that nobody else did. It wasn't a judgmental look. It looked like the man pitied her.

We arrived just in time for the most spectacular Black Sea sunset I've ever seen. The sea was absolutely astonishing with its fiery oranges and purples coming at me in waves. I felt weak in the knees and had to sit down.

My family was rarely vacationing nowadays, and the Black Sea was an expensive place, especially Primorsko, which at that point was still a small town full of traveling artists, touring Bulgarian communist aristocracy and plenty of East Germans and Russians. I fell in love with the place. It was colorful, mystical, unaffordable and yet accessible if you were okay with a little danger.

We walked all the way to the summer camp which was just outside Primorsko. I was curious about the old town and its surroundings, but Dora insisted that we followed the seashore on the way to a village school that in the summer doubled as an art camp. I obeyed and walked after her taking in the sites and feeling relatively happy despite the fact that the seashore was completely unwalkable at times. It was covered with slippery rocks and high cliffs with thorny bushes in-between. Little did we know that there was a reason why people walked through town rather than climb cliffs and waddle through thorn fields and ancient Roman ruins, and it wasn't just the difficult terrain. After the first mile or so, we climbed over a steep hill and saw something that would make any girl gasp for air. Just below the hill lay a nudist beach that was full of old wrinkled East German men enjoying the sunlight on their shrinking reproductive organs. Needless to say, they were very excited to see us.

Never in my life have I climbed cliffs so fast. Too bad Guinness World Records weren't there to see me and Dora running up the hills pretending we didn't hear the horny calls beneath us. I ran dragging my duffel bag through the thorns and pulling my skirt down as much as I possibly could until I almost tore it apart. After all, I've made the skirt myself and I was no professional. But I was lucky I had a skirt even if it was a piece of shoddy craftsmanship, because the men below looked like a tribe in search of human sacrifice. In two seconds, their big bellies rose above the ground, their fragile stick-legs bending, skin stretching over pointy bones and dry hairs moving slowly in the light summer breeze, and they ran after us shouting things in German. I pictured myself being pulled in a sea of sunburned flesh and dead sperm and ran through the bushes scratched and beaten until I came out on a dusty road in the middle of nowhere. Dora was already there gasping for air with a big smile on her face.

I wasn't much for prayers at that point in my life, but that evening, I prayed. We both did. We lifted our heads to the skies and thanked our young legs and our guardian angels for letting us escape. Dora said: "May there be beautiful young flesh between our legs tonight. Amen!" I giggled, and we started looking for road signs to the camp.

It took us more than an hour to get there. It was already twilight by the time we reached the small patch of grass behind the washrooms where we were supposed to sneak in. It was fairly easy, and apart from some suspicious looks from older students and a teacher, we didn't raise as much as a student guard's eyebrow. That was such a relief. I didn't know what I would do if my behavior points were taken away or, worst case scenario, if I got expelled. I'd probably die of shame, I thought. At that time, behavior points were taken away for not getting to school in time because your house was in the middle of a nasty neighbourhood, or smiling at a 1st of May march, or nervous giggling at a communist leader's funeral because you didn't even know what was happening when a teacher dragged you into a room full of crying first graders. It was a strange world where sleeping with a teacher and having old-man-fat-body nightmares for the rest of your life was somehow a better idea than smiling in a crowd.

Dora and I had to go our separate ways. We couldn't sleep in the same room because most rooms were tiny and there were students in them already. I ended up in July's bed and Dora managed to persuade the girls to lend her the extra mattress somebody's overprotective parents had brought in the day before. I had my clothes on for most of the night, and July and I only tried to have sex once. We talked about jazz for a while and then slept. It was pleasant but no more than that. There was no romance, no longing or trembling of hearts. There might have been, but I wasn't feeling any of it. Sleeping with a boy was just…different. At least, my body didn't ache afterwards, and I didn't have to rush out of an old dusty studio bed.

When I woke up, I found the bed and most of the camp empty. I must have overslept and missed breakfast. There was nobody around in the big school building and it felt slightly spooky, like being the only one left alive after an alien invasion.

It was nine o'clock already, but Dora was still sleeping. I could see her feet sticking out from a child-size mattress on the floor in the big dorm room by the library. For somebody so tall, she had surprisingly small feet, I thought and tiptoed around her looking for my toiletry bag. Her rug sack was nearly empty when we left Plovdiv so she offered to put some of my belongings in it. The blue trousers and the white jacket that Dad brought from Africa plus my black-laced undies were dear to me so they were staying in my bag permanently, but all that other stuff could go in Dora's bag. My hair couldn't be combed anyway so I only needed a scrunchie for that, or maybe a fork from the kitchen. Rest of it was easily replaceable with whatever was lying around. I was looking for my toothbrush, but I had some baking soda and a mint in my jacket pocket just in case.

Dora was snoring on the dorm room floor, looking fairly blissful. Feeling a bit lonely in the vast worn-out school dorms, I was seriously contemplating waking her up but decided that it probably wasn't the best decision after several days of very little sleep. Besides, she was quite unpleasant when she was tired or hungry, so waking her up was plain stupid.

There wasn't much to do in an empty school other than snoop around dipping into other people's belongings, which was something only Dora could do with a clean conscience, so I walked out of the building and started inspecting the grounds. Overlooking the unevenly paved schoolyard was an old oak tree, and underneath it, there was a donkey still strapped to a large wooden carriage. "Idiots…damn soulless idiots," I mumbled, annoyed at the donkey's owner who couldn't care less if that poor animal lived or died in the hot summer weather. Nobody in my family would ever dream of leaving an animal strapped to a heavy carriage on a hot day like this, I thought, then realised that they probably all would, shook my head in disgust and went forward to talk to the abandoned donkey in question.

The donkey wasn't bothered by the heavy carriage much, or so it seemed. He didn't even look at me when I reached out to pet his forehead. The skin between his ears was so soft that it made my eyes tear up in a sudden wave of emotion. But this moment of profound gratitude to nature that I was having didn't last very long. The big library door opened with a bang and out came a woman in her sixties. She had one of those '80s' chemically induced red tall hairdos and a blue janitor coat on. She ignored me for a while and then shouted, "Oi! Leave him alone!" I stood frozen pretending I was just observing the donkey out of curiosity. She smiled, shook her head and sat on a large rock next to the door to smoke. After chain-smoking for a while, the woman started waving at me. Not wanting to reveal my illegal presence at the camp, I acted 'normal' and followed her into the library hall.

For a moment, I thought that snoring Dora, tall-hair woman and I were alone on the school grounds. The woman wasn't the chatty type. She just handed me a mop and pointed to a suspiciously oily spot on the floor where an appliance of some kind must have stood just minutes before. One could see tracks from the thing being dragged away from its place towards a door behind a large library desk. And behind the desk, there was another woman. I didn't see her at first as she was quietly sitting behind a pile of books, almost blending into the dusty library walls.

I mopped and mopped, but the stupid oil stain remained exactly the same size, shape and color as when I started. After about ten minutes, I gave up and dropped the mop with a sigh. That's when I noticed the woman behind the books. She saw me staring at her and smiled.

"Did they leave you behind?"
"I don't know…I suppose so. Was…was there any breakfast this morning?"
"Yes, and it was utterly disgusting."

The woman smiled again, looked at me for a short moment and started sorting books in neat piles. It didn't look like she was following any alphabetical order. She opened the books, browsed through the pages, said 'hm', 'good one' or 'garbage' and divided them accordingly. The 'garbage' pile became frighteningly high very quickly, which apparently amused her. Every time she added a book to the garbage pile, she made a joyful squeaky sound. She turned around, looked at me and started tossing books against the wall like it was the most normal thing to do with books. One book after another would hit the wall and then land on the top of the uneven pile below.

"The softcover ones are no fun to throw. Hand me that thick Lenin, will you!"

She glanced at me and nodded towards a big red bundle of hardcover Lenin biographies. I never understood why there had to be so many of them. He only had one life, and it wasn't even a long life.

"What are you waiting for? Make yourself useful, will you…"
"I should probably get back and wake my friend up. We were supposed to go to the old town before everyone comes back from their field studies."
"Is she the one snoring on the floor next door?"
"Yes. Her name is Dora."

The woman started laughing, reached up above her head and pulled her ponytail up until her long grey hair came down like a sea wave.

"Dora you say? The name suits her. How old are you two?"
"I'm sixteen and she is sixteen and a half."
"Those halves mean a lot, do they?"
"I guess so…"

I wasn't sure if I enjoyed the woman's company. She scared me a little with her big baggy trousers, unruly grey hair and that weird uncontrollable laugh. Why doesn't she dye her hair? And what's with the corduroy?

I headed towards the door, but the woman ran in front of me and put her hand on my shoulder.

"Sorry, kid! I didn't mean to scare you. Do you want a cup of coffee? Don't worry about your friend. You can see the dorm door from behind that cabinet over there; I'll tell you when she wakes up."

"Is it instant…the coffee?"

"I'll get the Nescafé out just for you if you sit with me for a while. Deal?"

"Okay. But…"

"We'll keep an eye on your friend, I promise."

I remembered my illegal presence and sat down next to her behind the big pile of books. It didn't feel like I had a choice. Besides, I was dying for a cup of coffee, especially if it was posh instant.

"What's wrong with my clothes then?"

"N-n-n-nothing," I stuttered looking down, feeling utterly embarrassed for being caught judging her appearance. It really wasn't any of my business. I just didn't want to get in trouble for talking to this obviously crazy person.

"So…Why do you want to be an artist?"

"Who said I wanted to be an artist?"

It was a good answer to her question, I thought. I didn't know why I wanted to be an artist. Maybe I wanted to be something else, a doctor or a teacher perhaps but definitely not an oncologist like my mother. I couldn't imagine being responsible for helping thousands of people with cancer-infected bones, brains and breasts. I made that clear in a painting titled 'Breasts turning into salt'.

"You don't even know if you want to be an artist, do you? Don't tell me, your parents sent you to art school to become a teacher. But you don't like kids. People don't like kids unless they are raised to birth children, like breeding stock…you know, like those cows over there. Children are only interesting when they ask questions. That's what I think anyway. Do you ask questions? Don't tell me. You keep that stuff to yourself. You have to, you know…if you want to be an artist."

"I don't know really. Everything in my school seems crystal clear…there are no unknown coefficients. The teachers are repeating things that they've learned themselves, like nothing has happened in the decades in-between, like nobody is evolving. Questions are of no use to me."

"Oooo, 'coefficients' you say. Fancy words there! So, you are the kid with the fancy words then. Have you had sex yet?"

That question came out of nowhere. I have always been a terrible liar so I just said 'yes' and took a deep breath expecting a lecture. She didn't offer any, but the way she looked at me changed. Her eyes went soft and she stopped laughing. The craziness in her body language disappeared, like she had been acting the entire time. All of a sudden, it felt like I was talking to a long lost aunt or an older cousin.

"That whole sex thing is overrated. I've only had it once with this fat old artist in his studio. It was nothing special and I think that I might be allergic."

"Oh, honey, I hear you. That sex that you are talking about, that's overrated for sure. If you want to know anything about real heartfelt love and sex, talk to an old hag like me. Don't ask your mother or your grandmother. The only love they know is that of a tired horny sweaty drunk who would fuck anything that walks on two legs and sometimes four. Men are utterly useless which is why we are living in such a doomed hopeless society. I don't know how they came to be in charge, but it was the dumbest idea for sure."

She lit a cigarette, spread her arms and started drawing broad circles as if she was summarising our whole realm of existence. I felt increasingly anxious. I opened my mouth to contradict her, but something in me stopped the words from coming out. My own aunt was living proof that women could be shit too. So…are we all shit then? My whole body went cold, and in a split second, years of memories flashed before my eyes. Some were of my father and his friends mocking their wives for lying at the edge of the bed at night fully dressed in their thick long nightgowns. And some were memories of hiding under the kitchen table eavesdropping on my mother and her friends talking about how 'disgusting' their husbands were. There was the vivid memory of one woman describing what can only be a violent assault and another talking about almost losing her hearing because her husband enjoyed ejaculating in her ears. I felt so frightened that I started shaking.

The woman put her hands on my shoulders again and kept them there until I stopped shaking. I wanted that whole conversation gone so I turned to the book piles in front of us.

"Why are you piling them up like that?"

"I do that once a month just to see how much my perception of these books has changed over time. I've written it all down. See!"

"She pulled a small notebook from under her shirt and showed me notes dating back to 1969, the year of the moon landing."

"The moon landing was in 1969."

I was excited to see one set of numbers that I recognised. Rest of the numbers made no sense to me whatsoever. The woman ran her fingers through the neat columns in her notebook and laughed again.

"There are almost no books I like nowadays. I liked almost all of them in 1969. It's funny how it works."

There was a sudden thump and the main library door opened with a bang. Dora marched in looking visibly annoyed.

"Did you know that there is an animal strapped to a large heavy cart in the sun outside? Did you?"

She didn't wait for anyone to answer.

"Iva, get the fuck out of that chair and let's go! I'm hungry, and we are late for our ride to Sunny Beach. We have to look for the guy now. To the devil with him!"

I jumped off the chair, mumbled 'See you later' and followed Dora out.

"No, you won't see me. Do me a favour…don't do that communist crap art or that old lady art, you know, the flowers, pots and singing birdies bullshit. Paint

124

angry men or people who think…paint women who think for themselves. Promise me that you'll do something that matters and not some shit!"

"Okay, I won't."

"Have a good life and don't let them take you!"

Dora stopped marching and turned around.

"Who are 'them'?"

"I don't know what she means. She crazy."

"Yeah…"

20

We didn't find the boy that was supposed to take us to the infamous Sunny Beach resort. He was either a second cousin of Dora's or a distant relative of her father's and 'those were unreliable'. She was cursing him all the way through Old Primorsko until we ran into an acquaintance of my mother's. I wasn't supposed to be anywhere near the Black Sea and the young woman we met was training to be a nurse at Mom's hospital. I was as petrified as one might expect in such circumstances. It turned out she was faking the flu and wasn't supposed to be there either. We made a pact to never tell anyone.

I didn't know her first name so we called her 'nurse'. She was small and childlike, with soft features and big doll eyes adorned by the kind of long curled up eyelashes that every girl dreamed of. I was surprised at how witty and funny she was outside work. Dora seemed to like her enough so we went for coffee. All three of us wore patched-up short skirts, trunk tops and tennis shoes, which made us look like a trio from a traveling circus. She was a couple of years older than us, but it didn't seem to bother her at all. I think she liked the idea of me hitchhiking and hanging out at the Black Sea with her, as if by helping me she was revolting a little against the 'stiff' authority of my 'very proper' mother.

We had coffee and talked for an hour. I mostly sat and listened to the two of them talk. The young nurse confused me a little because I sensed a lightness in her that I hadn't seen in any of the women I knew. She didn't seem to care if things went wrong or something bad was happening, she just waved her hand as if to say 'Oh, it's nothing', smiled and marched ahead. I spent an hour listening to Dora trying to get sympathy from her for all our troubles on the way to Primorsko, from our money being halved, supposedly by Dora's father, to the wrinkly horny Germans that chased us up that cliff. She just smiled and said: "What an adventure!"

Dora expected people to engage with her and yet, she accepted little to no reaction from our new companion. I was walking along, listening to the two of them talk, almost hoping for Dora to cut the conversation short and pronounce the whole encounter meaningless. It was the sort of thing that made her a great friend, I thought. I waited for her lips to part and blur out a curse maybe, or a very impatient 'You are not listening to me. What do you think about Gorbatsjov and his Perestroika? Is he full of shit or what? We, the artists, will never be free.'

She did none of that.

I didn't join the conversation until we sat by the pier to eat lunch. We lined up by one of the many fish and chips shops by the beach and bought a cone of fried shrimp each. The tiny shrimp was deep-fried and poured in a paper cone made of old communist newspapers. We sat down by the edge of the marina and started eating out of our cones laughing at what the oil stains did to the faces of our 'beloved' communist leaders.

I heard myself go on and on about Dad's love for fishing and the amazing dishes he prepared for us when he came back from Africa. I really wanted to tell her about Troj, but the fear of receiving an awkward smile and a reprimand from Dora just wasn't worth the risk. Besides, she probably knew all the gossip considering where she did her practice. That place was like a hornet's nest, nothing and no one was safe from whispers in the yellow-painted hallways and the biased ears of patients dying for some kind of entertainment. I bet the gossip was vicious, but my mother would rather have the fruit of their poisonous tongues than their pity so she let them gossip, correcting them from time to time using one of her nurses as a proxy.

By the time we finished our shrimp, we had both fallen for the young nurse. That lightness of hers was something we both lacked, wanted and admired. Dora and I never stopped thinking and talking about painful things we experienced and felt, like we needed words to remain relevant in a world that didn't make any sense. It was almost like we were wired to relive everything and we couldn't stop ourselves. That wasn't how she was and that simple fact stunned us. We were very interested to know how she did it. We surrounded her like archaeologists waiting for a secret tomb door to open when the sun hit its highest point. She would tilt her head slightly and giggle, like she was flirting with us, fully aware that she was very attractive, and we would take short breaths and exhale in awe like we had just seen God smiling.

It didn't last long. We followed her to an exhaustingly boring party at a communist apparatchik's house, then ended up sleeping in a tent on the beach with boys poking at our breasts all night. Our young nurse was nowhere to be seen.

I woke up countless times during the night, half the time to fight off eager teenagers that were so drunk that they had to lean on the tent, and we all know what that looks like, and half the time because I was regretting going anywhere with Mom's apprentice. Dora's natural instincts would usually protect us from doing dangerously stupid things, but they seemed to evaporate in the nurse's presence.

My regret had very little to do with the things that the average teenage girl would normally regret, like being too flirtatious, drinking too much, or telling way too many people that my brother killed himself just when they were leaning over to kiss me. It was none of that specifically. I regretted the entire thing. I regretted being in that place, listening to the quasi-philosophical gibberish that was tossed back and forth like it was some kind of wisdom, knowingly exposing myself to countless reminders that I didn't belong, all because I thought I had just seen God smiling. But God wasn't smiling, she was just showing us what life could be for girls that weren't us and that was just cruel.

I believed in some kind of God, higher plane, fate, or whatever I might have called it throughout the years. In my 16-year-old mind, God was fate and fate had things in store for me, not all of them good, but some, like that box of candy that July brought to the hospital when I was sick, or the fact that by dying, Troj finally managed to get rid of our most annoying relatives and the pretend friends that always circled around my parents, for wine, food, cures for their illnesses or help with that porch that they were too lazy or stupid to fix on their own.

Trying to sleep in a hot smelly tent on the beach, fighting off boys all night and failing because there were simply too many of them and some were grown men, was painful, not in that purposeful way that would make a Grandma Kerana story complete but in the way that rendered things meaningless. Falling asleep felt like sinking in hot liquid sand.

When I woke up, I screamed so loud that Dora rushed from the other tent, struggled to unzip the front, couldn't open it all the way and literally fell through the thin fabric landing on my chest. Her protective instincts were back and that made me so happy that I started hugging her roughly like I was wrestling a bear. She punched me in the face.

We gathered whatever was left from our belongings and almost ran back to Primorsko Old Town. Dora was famous for not discussing rough nights, but I could definitely tell that there was enough tension in the air to change her mind about the benefits of sharing. She walked as if her skirt was on fire, with long

128

quick steps as if she was marching in an imaginary squad, in a life-and-death situation. Just before the medieval town wall, she suddenly stopped and turned around. I was gasping for air after running after her for almost a mile.

"Jesus Almighty, those boys were dumb!"

"They sure were," I agreed, nodding in breathless frenzy.

"Did you see the one with the tiny goatee? He was the dumbest of them all, but they all flocked around him like he was some kind of preacher. A beard doesn't make a philosopher, don't they get that? His wasn't even a beard…it was ten hairs in a bundle like the hair between my legs, if that…What a dick!"

"He thought I was 'adorable'. What an arse!"

"I'm starving. You hungry? I don't think we have any money left apart from the emergency stash."

Oddly enough, our money was untouched. There it was, ladies and gents, the one perk in following communist aristocracy around – you get to keep your money. For the first time on this trip, my friend and I waved our hands as to say 'We really don't care' and left the beach, tents, nurse, goatee man, handsy boys and pseudo-intellectual gibberish behind like they never existed and went on a hunt for pancakes.

The neatly paved alley leading to the old town square had artists already lining up to sell their drawings, paintings and various creatures made of seashells. If Dora didn't have my wallet in her back pocket, I would have spent all my money on seashell animals. Mom would so love at least ten of them to spread around her beautiful improvised balcony garden.

Being an art school student at one of the two top art schools in the country, I thought I would recognise most of the artists there. I didn't see anyone familiar, not even the cousin or sibling of anyone I knew. Dora was one year above me and seemed to know more people than I did, so shortly after we arrived, she abandoned the hunt for pancakes and started running from artist to artist exchanging travel tips and gossip. I had little choice but to follow her around nodding and pretending I knew people.

After running around for a while, Dora stopped to talk to a young man she seemed to like a lot. She was flirting with him, which was something I hadn't seen her do in a long time, if ever. It soon became clear that he too was a student at our school. Dora was telling him about our first night in Primorsko, mentioning the art camp outside town, when he nodded with a smile and said:

"I bet the teachers knew that you were there without permission, but they let you stay because of her."

I stepped back a couple of steps in dismay. What he was saying didn't make any sense. Dora was puzzled too.

"Why would they? You've been at the school for four odd years now, you know how much they like punishing us."

"Everyone is tiptoeing around her because of what happened in her family."

My mouth opened in an expression that probably looked like something Edvard Munch painted. I pushed Dora to the side and heard myself shouting like a banshee.

"NOTHING happened in my family. Something happened with all of us individually. Troj happened and then all of you happened, you miserable dickless...incompetent...retarded...ugly PEDOS! By the way, you are cheating. Look everyone, this guy is CHEATING! These are not original drawings but colored XEROX COPIES. I can tell because there is no variation in the ink. NO VARIATION..."

When I started walking past the small crowd that was now gathering, I expected somebody to run after me, but nobody did. I walked and walked until I realised that Dora still had my money. I walked back, pretending to be unaware of the hundred people staring at me, pushed Dora to the side again, reached in her back pocket, took my wallet and left.

That day, I took the bus to Ivanka's house. I never saw Dora again.

The house was just as I last saw it, dark and cool upstairs, hot and dusty downstairs, garden full of flowers, animals and birds, and the vines protecting us all from the hot orange disk in the sky.

Ivanka wasn't expecting me. She looked puzzled for a split second and started crying. I sat on a wobbly chair under the vines and waited for her to calm down. She mumbled and shook her head. Then she started whispering looking awkward as if she wasn't sure of the meaning of her words.

"It's been months since I saw you last...months."

"I haven't been here since that horrible New Year's Eve, I suppose. What have you been up to, Grandma?"

It was strange how easy it was to talk to her all of a sudden. It felt odd at first, but then I realised that this was the first time we were alone since my toddler years, and it felt surprisingly comfortable.

"Same old, same old, I suppose, right? You look well, Grandma."

She smiled a very careful shy smile and sat down opposite my chair. Her hands curled up in her lap and her shoulders relaxed. The smile grew a little bit wider.

"Same old, same old, as you said. Did you just get back from camp? Where was it this summer?"

"The Asenovgrad tin factory. Can't you smell the tomatoes on me? I bet I still smell of rotten export tomatoes."

"I can warm up the water for you if you want to take a shower."

"I went to the Black Sea with a friend, but Mom and Dad have no idea that I did that so please don't say anything! I know you tend to say things without thinking much, but don't throw me under the bus if you care about me. Please!"

She made a sign with her hand suggesting she wouldn't say a word, and I told her everything about Dora and her father who stole our money and beat her every chance he got; about the trip in the truck, the Germans, the nurse and her pseudo-intellectual friends, our night on the beach fighting off boys, the pain in my backside that made it almost too painful to walk the day after and our morning in Primorsko Old Town. Whatever happened didn't visibly hurt me so it didn't matter. Right?

Her facial expression shifted throughout the story, from various levels of amusement to sheer horror and then back to amusement. Slight twitching occurred from time to time and her hands appeared to be sweating in discomfort, but she didn't say anything, just listened and nodded.

When I was done talking, my grandmother brushed the hair off my face and got on her feet. She dusted herself off and walked towards the summer kitchen to make me a snack. I ate the surprisingly tasty pancakes she made for me, climbed the stairs to the cool part of the house and slept for a whole day and a half.

21

That summer turned out to be a surprisingly good one. After sleeping the whole Jack Kerouac experience off, I wrote 'prick' on the cover of the book, stashed it in an old drawer beneath the sink, washed my clothes and got ready to leave.

Ivanka's behavior was slightly odd but felt somehow appropriate. She hardly said a thing after our conversation, mostly tiptoed around me with fear in her eyes and fulfilled my every wish however busy she was. I had never seen her behave like this before and an ounce of pity found its way around my anger and annoyance to make leaving her behind hard and awkward. For the first time, it occurred to me that she was all alone in this big old brick house full of memories of people now gone. I mumbled, "See you soon, Grandma," and marched out on the street without closing the door. She followed me out and stood there watching me walk away.

Tracia welcomed me in its usual manner, with loud gossipers sitting on benches switching topics as soon as I passed them by, old women leaning over balconies making clicking sounds with their tongues at the sight of my handmade short skirt and my dad making his twentieth attempt to paint over some local graffiti around our entrance of Block 23.

Dad didn't say much either. He turned around, smiled and handed me one of his painting brushes. I dipped it in the paint, made one long stroke and handed it back to him.

"I am tired, Dad. Is Mom home?"
"Yeah, she sure is. Go! I just wanted a maestro's touch on my new piece."
"It's not new, is it though?" I said laughing and ran up the stairs.

Running up the stairs had become a habit of mine. Our neighbours seemed to think that I was being wasteful and ungrateful since we had an elevator and an elevator was apparently one of the comforts Communism provided for its workers and as such had to be used when available. Fair point I assumed. Old townhouses that used to belong to the rich before they were confiscated, like the one Rosie lived in, had no elevators so one could probably say that it was a perk, but I preferred the stairs anyway. It wasn't because of the exercise. A month or so before Troj died, I did something stupid. I was trying to eavesdrop on Troj and Brother while hiding in the elevator but my fingers slipped and I let the heavy metal door close. Somebody on the upper floors pressed the button and the old panel-clad Russian box that was our elevator started moving upwards with my school uniform and me attached to it. In desperation, I grabbed a gym shoe and jammed it between the elevator and the wall. The elevator stopped with a screeching sound so loud that I lost my hearing for a moment. Imagining my very sad funeral and wondering what kind of flowers my mother would pick to put above my head in the coffin, I suddenly remembered Dad mentioning an emergency handle on the side. I pulled the first thing that matched that description. When the door opened, I crawled out and ran up the stairs before anyone could see me. Perk or no perk, from that day on, I rather stay outside forever than use the damn thing.

Mom was baking something that made the whole building smell of butter cookies. I was expecting some kind of reprimand for being away for so long, but she said nothing. I had lied to them for months just so I could go on a road trip with Dora, and I got away with it. It didn't really matter anymore because my parents would never know. The school had next to no contact with them due to a common belief that once a child was trusted upon the system it belonged to it indefinitely.

That evening we spent several hours just chatting and tasting the various dishes Mom had prepared. The obligatory Russian movie was on, which usually meant watching the television set with the sound muted, but this time, the sound was on full blast.

The only movie on National Television that evening was an adaptation of Alexandre Dumas' book, *The Three Musketeers*. It was clever, funny and the actors were 'unusually attractive for Russians' as Dad put it making a ticking sound with his tongue at the sight of the Russian actress playing Queen Anne of France. I stretched myself on the sofa keeping an eye on young Mikhail Boyarsky's interpretation of D'Artagnan thinking it wasn't that bad apart from the occasional bursting into loud Russian song. The song and the typical knee-clapping dance made these very French characters a lot less convincing, but the rest of it was nice. Dari was sleeping in the bedroom, and I was told not to wake her up. I was enjoying this evening with Mom and Dad and although a small part

134

of my brain was still fidgeting about the blood spilled on the very same spot where my head was resting, I was sort of…happy.

22

School started in September with a new set of classes and teachers. Not all of it made sense, but I was slowly getting onboard with the idea that sacrifices must be made and appearances must be kept.

One of the big changes was the introduction of military training as a whole day experience. It was dumb and exhaustingly theoretical, which meant long hours of listening to ideological nonsense just so I could enjoy ten minutes of target practice. The only good thing about it was that it replaced PE, which I disliked disturbingly much. Physical Education at my art school was 'taught' by a retired Olympian gymnast who hated herself and her life to such a degree that it permeated everything she said and did. She systematically tortured every young girl that she considered 'pretty and entitled'. I couldn't disagree more regarding this categorisation of my humble demeanour, but I was unmistakably her main target. She had me running around the schoolyard in tiny shorts, flapping my arms like a chicken in front of the whole school, doing push-ups that I couldn't really do despite some documented desperate trying and made everyone in my class line up using my breasts as measure. My only consolation was the thought that chances were she would die a lonely angry spinster with bleached hair and inverted chest, with her green plastic whistle still stuck in her teeth.

The first day of military training was disappointing. We were briefly introduced to the parts of a typical Kalashnikov AK 47 and just as I stretched my arms to embrace the shiny machine gun, the teacher put it aside and burst into Communist bravado.

"We must learn the spirit of absolute selflessness. With this spirit, everyone can be very useful. A man's ability may be great or small, but if he has this spirit, he is already pure, a man of moral integrity and above vulgar interests, a man who is of great value to The People."

"Sorry...can I see that machine gun again? Pleeeease!"

"No...hands on the table! What's your name?"

"Iva."

"Sit up, you ungrateful midget!"

I had never been called 'midget' before and had no idea what it meant as an insult so my hands were placed on the table and my mouth shut closed as he continued.

"All men must die, but death can vary in its significance. To die for The People is weightier than a mountain, but to work for imperialists and fascists and die for the exploiters and oppressors is lighter than an atom. To die for The Party means to die for The People. If we have shortcomings, we are not afraid to have them pointed out and criticised, because we serve The People. Anyone, no matter who, may point out your shortcomings. If he is right, We, The People will correct them. Do you understand me?"

I definitely didn't. I could honestly say that I never expected to be taught a class in death when I woke up that particular morning. And yet here we were talking about dying for The Party. The thought of such death made my skin crawl. I could almost hear the voices above my head in the grave: "She was born the daughter of a woman who grew up in an orphanage and a man who wanted to be an inventor but wasn't. She was a horrible sister who failed to protect her little brother. Her teeth and breasts were too big for her size, and she really should have worn those braces. She only managed to have sex with a man once, and it turned out she was allergic to his sperm or beard or something. Her life was cut too short because she died for a thing, and because of death for a thing, she couldn't find time to do better than we already said. Let's have lunch!"

That evening, I spent hours wandering around Plovdiv Old Town thinking about this six-millennia old place and how insignificant it all was in comparison. I touched the stones of old houses, counted the bricks of a majestic arch (1376 including two or three missing) and sat on the ancient stones of a Roman amphitheatre on the top of a hill. That AK 47 was the only thing I could think of after a while. Contemplation doesn't always yield results for me.

Just as I was standing up ready to go, slightly dizzy from sitting on the top of some very steep stairs, I heard a voice behind me.

"You don't have to leave on account of us. Please stay!"

137

I turned around and saw a whole group of students emerging from a building behind the amphitheatre. The sign above the main entrance spelled 'Music Academy' in golden letters in neat Times Roman font, quite adequate for the building's location, I thought. The boy talking to me was in the centre of the group. He was handsome, slim and somewhat taller than me. He must have been four or maybe five years older. He sat next to me and put his books between us. I sat back down, looked at my feet and mumbled.

"I have to get home. It will get dark soon and the bus to Tracia is less than reliable."

"Well…that means we have just about an hour and forty minutes then."

He smiled at me and stood up.

"We are going to my friend D's house to play some piano. You can come and listen for a while if you want. My name is T. This is N and this awkward looking guy there is Mr O."

"I'm Iva and I prefer to be called by my whole name if that's okay."

He smiled again and started walking down the steep stairs and across the amphitheatre to the other side of the hill. I somehow assumed that they were all boys so I said, "No, thanks," and started walking in the other direction. Seconds later, I heard a woman's voice.

"Hi! I'm D. I know you. You gave me one of your pears once. We were both sitting underneath the trees in front of the cinema, and you thought I looked hungry. That was kind of you."

She seemed friendly enough, but I didn't remember her. I must have given away enough pears that day to feed a village.

D's house was a lot farther than I thought. I didn't know any of these people so I took a cigarette out of T's packet and pretended to smoke. They were all really good-looking, I thought, especially T, who wouldn't stop smiling at me. It made me giggle, and for the first time in ages, I felt comfortable giggling away. These people were strangers. They knew nothing about me and my family. To them, I was just an artist in training who didn't know how to smoke, lived in

Tracia, wore a school uniform and had a sculpting knife in her backpack in case of art, emergencies or paedophile encounters happening.

D's room was on the top floor of a five-storey building and appeared to be an old electrician's room from back in the days when machine rooms and elevator rooms came with an electrician. It was small but cosy, with a window ceiling and doves nesting on top of it behind a giant chimney. I decided that sooner or later I would be moving in.

The small group sat around the room and continued their conversation. They were arguing about music, mainly Stravinsky, making jokes about their teachers and mocking D who apparently failed her piano exam.

My presence in that room was barely noticeable, which is understandable considering the other people there were at least five years older, had their own rooms and were already in college. And besides, what did I know of Stravinsky? I spent most of the now 40 minutes left to departure smiling and nodding like I was part of the conversation.

After a while, the room started spinning. Remembering Dad's drinking rules, I got up, holding my head with both hands and zig-zagged to the tap outside to get water. The narrow dark corridor led to two separate rows of attic storage rooms separated by chicken wire, and between the first two doors, there was a broken sink with a rusty but functional tap. I drank some water, looked in a piece of an old cracked mirror glued to the wall and decided that my blurry face was pretty enough to enter the room again.

D had stopped playing the piano. The room was filled with cigarette smoke, and they were all sitting on cushions on the floor talking. An out of tune guitar emerged from somewhere and N started playing and singing Vysotskij songs. I heard myself saying that Vysotskij is probably the only thing you can play on an out of tune guitar. Everybody laughed, and D handed me a bottle of beer.

I was once again…happy.

I moved in a week later. The floor D and I shared was a partially rebuilt attic, and Dad was not impressed with the uneven ceilings, walls, windows and especially the sink and tap ordeal. It was shoddy craftsmanship indeed, and he disapproved. But he had listened to me going on and on about the benefits of having my own studio for just about the entire long Saturday morning so I thought I'd let him have the pleasure of pointing at faulty fittings and shaking his head for at least an hour or so.

We dragged some old furniture up the stairs. Dad walked around shaking his head some more to no vain. I sat on the floor, opened a can of purple paint and started painting a chair. The strong smell of turpentine filled the room and caused my father to wave at his nose. He opened the big ceiling window, mumbled, "Don't even think about being late for supper," and left the room.

23

A lot of new things happened in that room. That kiss T gave me was new. Making love was also new. And there were even more new things attached to the other new things. Like closing one's eyes to take it all in and feel pleasure rather than living in forced blindness because of an overactive brain. At that point in my young life, I hadn't experienced anything but what Mom and her friends referred to as 'the old in-and-out' with some superficial kissing, most of the time without tongues. T was a flute player and kissing him was like going to the school of actually enjoying things. That was truly new.

Meeting T's parents was new too. His mother embraced me with such warmth that I started wondering if she could be my substitute parent for a while, at least as long as I was dating her son. I wasn't exactly looking for more parents, I just thought that some variety could be good for my health.

I was really missing Troj. I wanted to talk about all the new things, in the way we used to do in our improvised bed under the covers, fiddling with pocket knives and blushing intensely. It was mostly me who blushed, by the way. He would giggle and tease, but I would tell him things anyway because he was mine.

I so wanted to once again blush, talk and then listen and laugh at his silly and somewhat cynical remarks while poking him with a plastic sable. Even if it was just in my head. But the grim summer, that stupid trip to the Black Sea, the whole Manasi ordeal and my ever decreasing self-worth had made all the imaginary conversations impossible. How could one discuss such misery-inducing things? Like a woebegone dullard that doesn't respect the dead and their privacy. My wish was to tell him about feeling alive and wanting to write poetry and paint portraits again, this time without blood-red stains and black teeth.

It was hard because almost two years had gone and I still couldn't make heads or tails of Troj's violent death. Whenever I wanted to shout 'Damn you...' in my head or otherwise, there was no name or word to put in place of the dotted line. What happened? Was it him wanting to end it all? Why? Dad was due back from Africa and there were going to be amazing foreign-looking presents and a whole lot of wonderful stories told in the way that only our father could, with witty embellishments and jokes that took a while to figure out so one would wake up in the middle of the night laughing because one finally got it.

Did somebody murder Troj or forced him to pull the trigger? Who? How was all that connected to the strange incident with the watch? Who or what was Troj running from that day? Why did his friend 'Brother' disappear without saying a word? Where did he go?

I had things to tell him – new things that were worth the risk of waking up the dead. But it was hard considering how many thoughts I had ignored or stored away for later days. With all these questions lingering, silence was understandable. Even when conversations were imaginary.

It wasn't all about him.

There were other things that I couldn't possibly speak of, in my head or otherwise. They were enormous and disturbing. They were the kind of things that people didn't even whisper about in their sleep…terrifying inexplicable things. Like that time in our young lives when Dad ceased being Dad. It didn't last long, but it left me and Troj wondering if our lives were changing in a way that we couldn't possibly control. And that, ladies and gentlemen, was carving things in stone to last beyond the grave.

It was the sum of all things, I suppose: the incessant fighting in our families with Eunice and Ivanka winning all the battles after Grandpa Troj died; the fact that we had no money; the fact that we never had any money; the never-ending bickering between Troj and I; and maybe the biggest one of all – the fact that their marriage was in a bad shape. Dad grew bitter, colder and angrier with everyone and everything. Eventually, he started to resemble the men that he drank beer with, the same men that mocked their wives for sleeping on the edge of the marital bed and hated them and the children. We were hoping that this was a phase, and at some point, with Mom's help, he would go back to being our Dad again. We were hoping for a speedy recovery.

Thing was, Mom wasn't helping. She started sleeping on the edge of the bed in a heavy all-enveloping nightgown until they were fighting every night and Dad was expelled to the kitchen sofa. That was when his impressive collection of bottled rakia and cognac, neatly kept in a cabinet next to the TV, was replaced by a river of cheap liquor. (One thing that you might not know about communism: no matter how bad the economy was and how empty the store shelves were, there always was an unlimited supply of cheap liquor.)

142

I didn't care that much about my inability to walk after being kicked to the ground in some kind of rage that wasn't my fault. And Dad was a strong kicker. I cared even less than that about the petty bickering between them two. What scared me and Troj the most was the fact that Mom was changing too.

She stopped eating and started chain-smoking. Chores at home and projects at work were stripped to the bare minimum of what was required for fitting within the standard description of 'parent' and 'citizen'. It became harder and harder to be around her. Patients and hospital staff would circle around her in fear which, of course, generated a whole new set of problems. And she loved her work so none of this made any sense. Chores that she usually enjoyed became burdens and bills started piling up at a rate never before seen in our household. And our parents were proud bill-payers.

When Dad tried to pull himself together and reset the clock, so to speak, Mom answered with blame and resentment, not for the things he did then and there but for past sins that didn't even sound like sins at all. She started blaming him for everything, her chain-smoking, sleepless nights and lost appetite included, like it was all his fault and she had nothing to do with any of it.

Like the screaming, chaos, alcohol and chain-smoking weren't enough, there was also the puppy incident.

It wasn't Troj's fault really, he wasn't the one that found the puppies. Although, in the name of honesty, he was the one that decided to take them in. There were three of them. They were newborn and their mother was nowhere to be seen. Maybe somebody tied a rock around her neck and drowned her as one might do with a dog if one was a soldier from the barracks behind the Tracia forest. The puppies were all brown with darker spots here and there and pink tightly shut eyes. Every child on the block agreed that they were 'breathtakingly cute', and it was suggested by my brave but somewhat foolish little brother that we take them home to our flat on the sixth floor of 23 G.

We spent that whole afternoon on the platform between the sixth and the fifth floor playing with the puppies. Most of the neighbourhood children came to play at one point or another, between late lunches and suppers, but by the time Mom came home after a morning shift in the hospital, it was just Troj, me and 'Slow Kid' from next door.

We saw Mom get off the bus, and just as precaution, hid the puppies behind a storage door. That proved to be absolutely meaningless because all the gossipers and snitches were out on their balconies at this point, and she was thoroughly informed about all of it: the puppies, where and when they were found and who brought 'them darn fleabags' in the building. That would be Troj, may I remind you.

"We will see about that," she said and entered the building. She didn't seem angry or worried, just annoyed that we didn't make sure that the puppies were 'safe to play with'. "Can I look?" she asked. We produced the puppies with glee and assured her that they were indeed 'safe to play with'. She looked at our arms and bare legs searching for flea bites but didn't see any, then said 'Hm', walked up to the flat and closed the door behind her.

We didn't see Dad coming, but we heard his steps in the bottom of the stairs. After all this time living with the man, we knew exactly what that sounded like. He didn't wait for the elevator but walked up the five flights of stairs with what sounded like rapid jumps. When he reached the platform underneath us, it felt like the building trembled. Voices echoed in the corridor. Once again, the gossipers and snitches were making sure that Dad knew every detail of the puppy 'ordeal'. He didn't say anything witty and funny back to them as he would usually do but continued in our direction. That scared the life out of us three, even 'Slow Kid'.

We expected a big fight but none happened. Dad walked past us without even looking and told us to make a home for the puppies somewhere else. This strange behavior felt disturbingly ominous. We would rather have the fight, we thought, even if strong Dad legs were involved.

We laid an old blanket on the floor of the storage room and left the door slightly ajar with bricks on each side to keep the puppies from sneaking out. We asked Mom if we could keep our front door open to check on the puppies now and then, but she wouldn't have it. "It's not that kind of neighbourhood," she said.

I couldn't fall asleep that evening and neither could Troj. Our parents seemed fast asleep behind the closed, and probably locked, bedroom door.

Just after midnight, I heard a sound, tiptoed to the front door, pressed my ear to the cold metal and listened hoping to hear puppies. I didn't hear anything so I tried looking through the peephole. That wasn't exactly easy. After a late night visit from Ivanka's nephew Genjo, so drunk he couldn't stand up straight to save his life, Dad had enforced the door with a metal frame. The frame was still rough and uneven with sharp edges sticking out and poking me in the ribs. But there I was, hugging the door, keeping an eye out for puppy-related things and whimpering quietly in the dark. Suddenly, a dark shadow appeared out of nowhere. There was a dull sound and then nothing. Terrified, I ran back to my bed and covered my face with the heavily soap-scented summer duvet.

That morning, three small piles of guts and fur appeared on the ground below our balcony. Troj leaned over the concrete balcony front and stared at the piles. He teared up but didn't cry. He just couldn't believe it.

We never thought or spoke of this again.

One day, Dad just left. He packed a small suitcase in the car, filled his big metal thermos with coffee and went fishing.

Being left alone, Mom felt confused. There was nobody to blame all of a sudden. She tried blaming us but that just didn't sound right. We couldn't possibly be blamed for 'messing with the TV with our stupid little screwdrivers'. We didn't have screwdrivers. We could borrow some from Dad, but they wouldn't be ours, would they?

Troj couldn't be blamed for not washing his clothes or stacking the bills underneath the pile of old newspapers so that 'nobody could ever find them'. Troj had very little knowledge of washing machines, especially the Lithuanian kind we had, and couldn't tell an electricity bill from a September the 9th remembrance card.

After a week or so of weirdness and confusion, Mom decided to better herself. She started to count her cigarettes and go to bed early instead of watching TV until midnight and then hanging wet clothes on the balcony until two o'clock just so that she could tell us about it in the morning. She was becoming more agreeable at work so the hospital staff stopped making big circles around her in fear, just small cautious ones. Before long, she was eating better and swimming again with her friend Nata at the Plovdiv Central Bath House. Once a week, like before. They weren't swimming really, just bobbing around in the water like two wet but colorful decorations.

When Dad finally showed up and unloaded the car in absolute silence, she went into the bedroom and closed the door. She wasn't hiding, just watching him from the bedroom balcony wondering how much of that trip was about fish.

Dad was tanned, clean and all too well-dressed and handsome for somebody who had supposedly spent a month crouching around the lakes in his rubber boots.

We were told to get out of the flat immediately.

As said, it didn't last long, just as long as it took to suffer a hard enough blow to a belief system based on love and safety being a given in our family. Whatever memories were made then, remained buried for decades, all but the one about the fishing trip that saved the family. That memory was good. We brought it up whenever Mom and Dad started bickering. Once or twice, we dragged the fishing rod out for them to see and be reminded.

T and I became the couple that everyone thought was unbreakable. Wherever we went, people were telling us how well we fit together. Some thought that it was because 'art and music were a natural fit', like we were somehow art and music personified. What a ridiculous notion, I thought, but the flattery didn't escape me. Whatever it was that made us good together worked very well for a brief moment in time.

There was only one person that didn't seem very happy.

D became more irritable with every friendly couple-related gesture or comment aimed at me and T. Whether people smiled at us or complemented us on our compatibility, she reacted with contempt. She was very friendly with each of us individually but not when we were together. This made me anxious because I really liked her. The more her mood fluctuated, the more I wished to be near her. The more I was near her, the closer I wanted to get to her.

After about a month of the happy new couple frolicking on the streets of Plovdiv holding hands, D and I had a fight. It was one of those fights where nonsensical and yet hurtful things were said. I don't remember saying anything particularly nasty other than sarcastically apologising to her for her own 'inadequate hysteria'. She answered with the uncalled for: "You are like a magpie jumping through hoops just to get to that shiny new thing." The shiny thing being T. Did she mean that I didn't love him? I wasn't sure. It was quite obvious that she had a thing for him.

We didn't talk to each other for a long time, not because we were so incurably mad at each other but because neither of us knew what to say. T failing at meddling in our affairs again and again was truly painful to watch.

It wasn't T's persistence that brought us together at the end, it was our mutual hatred for gossipers and snitches, and to some extent, fear.

Your average professional snitch lived in a multi-storey building. If the snitch was female, it was highly likely that she was an elderly woman who shared her home with a spoiled son, a reluctantly submissive, possibly tormented daughter-in-law and a couple of noisy but invisible children. If the snitch was of the male persuasion, then he most probably lived with his mother and spent most of his time hiding behind curtains drooling at teenage girls like me. Our snitch was of the male persuasion.

He was fat and balding and lived with his mother who happened to be our landlady. The mother was in her early fifties, give or take. She was as skinny as your average yo-yo dieting, chain-smoking communist apparatchik's wife. It was hard to imagine that they were ever related. He must have been about twenty-two or twenty-three, but his thinning hair, swollen eyes and big belly, combined with the stained tracksuits he always wore, made him look much older than that. It was the constant lurking that made his eyes swell, I thought. Standing behind curtains with one hand holding a bottle of beer and the other permanently stuck in his pants did the rest.

He almost never spoke to me or D, but he followed us around a lot. The one incident when he went grabby pretending to bump into us two in the dark corridor connecting our rooms (a huge mistake that he lived to regret), ended with D punching him in the groin and me marching downstairs to report to his mother. My strategy didn't work because his mother wasn't home and the effect of my threat wore off given I couldn't follow up on it. D smirked while watching me fail, but snitch's actions must be punished so she showed him what it would look like if she was to shove a dead rat into his mouth and cut his penis off. Using some kind of thug sign language, she made it clear that his life would be over if he so much as glanced at me or her. He left us alone. For a while.

T becoming my official boyfriend opened a whole new world of opportunities for the snitch to do damage. In the '80s (not the disco-filled '80s you know and love but the communist version), sex was illegal for people under eighteen even if it was consensual and parent-approved. Typically for a totalitarian regime worth its label, the ban excluded the state-run trafficking apparatus that ensured the constant supply of young innocent flesh whenever a communist comrade felt horny.

One early morning, T and I were woken up by a loud banging on the studio door. A policeman in full military gear was standing on the other side hitting the door with his fist before announcing himself. T jumped into his trousers and threw a summer dress at me. I got dressed in two seconds and sat on the floor pretending to draw on a large piece of paper. The policeman stepped through the door as T opened, kicked it in T's face and placed his left boot on the right corner and his right boot on the left corner of the doorway, blocking the exit with his

Kalashnikov. "I'm not going anywhere, officer, we have nothing to hide," T said smiling.

"It's Captain Christof to you," he replied and stared at us sternly.

Fortunately, that particular policeman was quite young and willing to relate to our situation seeing T and he were roughly the same age. He hadn't realised that this was an artist studio, he said and had a look at some of my drawings, nodding approvingly.

The second T closed the door behind him, I started crying. It wasn't because I was scared (which I was) but because I had to explain everything to my father and persuade him to go to the police station to verify my identity and assure the authorities regarding parental approval of T's genitals entering my young body. T was older so he didn't have to do anything. My fear gave way to envy which turned into anger, and I cried some more.

That's when D knocked on the door. She had heard everything and wanted to help so she offered to go to the police station with both our passports and pretend that she was my cousin. I stopped crying.

That night, I called my parents and told them to 'come and get me'. I knew that our car was in the shop, getting its brakes fixed. Besides, it was Dad's football night with his drinking buddies so I assumed he was watching TV while polishing a bottle of freshly brewed rakia. It was the sort of thing I would do if I didn't want them to 'come and get me' while asking them to do exactly that.

Dad answered. After the initial 'Hmmm', the phone was handed to Mom. I heard: 'It's your daughter' and Mom walking towards the phone muttering something about D being 'a filthy thief'. With Dad busy having a good time with his band of delinquents and our car getting its brakes fixed, the only thing she could possibly do was to yell at me. That she did for a good five minutes, then sighed and ordered me to 'lock the door properly, get up in time in the morning, and come home directly after school the next day'.

D and I spent the evening listening to old records and chatting about politics and art. After drinking a bottle and a half of wine, we fell asleep in D's bed.

I woke up in the middle of the night paralysed with fear. D was awake too. She was staring at me in the dark and her hand was moving up and down my arm. That triggered some kind of knee-jerk reaction and I jumped. It wasn't unpleasant, just very sudden and strange. I went out of my way to explain to her that I was startled and 'that's all there was', but she shook her head, turned around and stared at the wall until morning.

The next day, I finished school earlier than usual and headed towards the studio hoping to patch things up with D. I was walking up the first set of stairs when a neighbour appeared out of nowhere, grabbed me by the arm and whispered, "What is going on up there at yours?" I had no idea what she was talking about, but there were strange sounds coming from the attic. Whether it was a thing or a creature that made those noises, it sounded frantic, to say the least.

I found D sitting at the top of the stairs waiting for me.

"Don't go in there!"
"Why not?"

She shook her head and looked down without answering.

The loud noises were clearly coming from my studio. It sounded like the voices of many different people. "More than a dozen men," I said to myself. Suddenly, the door flew open with a bang and a naked man with the biggest erection I had ever seen ran past me and towards the water tap at the bottom of the corridor.

A wave of adrenaline washed over me. I ran through the hallway and lashed at the door. The air in the room was stuffy and pungent with heavy smells – a mixture of sperm, rubber, dust but also alcohol and dirt. My studio was full of naked men. In the middle of the group, there was a heap of skin and bones that resembled a child or a very small woman. At first, I couldn't tell. Time stood still for a while, and after ten seconds or so, the body in the middle started opening up to show its distorted face. She raised her hand, brushed a lock of henna-dyed hair behind her right ear and looked at me with a cold stare. She was smiling. Smiling!

I screamed and shouted at the men until they were all gone. The words flying out of my mouth were obscene, harsh and clear and I must have created quite a stir for them to disperse so quickly. I have no recollection of who those men were. I wasn't looking at them. They were nothing but a ball of skin, hair and erections, with a girl in the middle.

The men left and peace was temporarily restored. It was just us there – two females looking at each other with confusion and D hiding behind her opened door in the corridor.

Yes, D? What was her role in all this? Nobody else but she knew where my second key was. Who were the men? Who let them in?

There was no way I could deal with this mess without Mom.

I had to somehow drag that girl out of the building and hail us a taxi, but she had nothing to wear but rags. I had taken all my clothes home to wash them, including my secret underwear stash, so I kicked D's door open while holding the girl by her left arm and dragging her across the corridor, grabbed a dress from the nightstand and forced it on the girl's cold skinny body. She put up a fight screaming 'Leave me alone, you ugly frigid bitch' accentuating the word 'frigid', but instead of letting go of her, I kept pulling the dress down until her body was all covered.

The taxi ride to Tracia was such an ordeal that the fact that we arrived at our final destination physically unharmed shocked me. I didn't have enough money to pay the driver. I was counting on my father being outside the building watering the plants so I could empty his pockets and take his beer money. He wasn't anywhere to be seen. I started counting coins, apologising to the driver while looking at D sternly. She took out some money, and we paid just enough to cover the bill. We made sure it was exactly the right amount, down to the last copper stotinka. Gratitude becomes obsolete in situations involving Romani girls reeking of bodily fluids and the omnipresent undercurrent of Plovdiv taxi drivers who lived to humiliate these girls. That being so, no gratuity was given, monetary or verbal.

We ran up to the flat hoping to remain unseen, but surely in a building full of gossipers and snitches, two young females dragging a Romani child up the stairs would be too juicy to ignore. We were not only seen but vigorously discussed for about a year, give and take.

Mom took a quick sharp look at us, and we were seated at the kitchen table where she could keep an eye on us while hovering over the kitchen top, making coffee and contemplating her reaction. We had some explaining to do so we couldn't stay silent for long. We started talking over each other, voicing concerns and tossing statements that made little sense as none of us had been given the time to mull over the events preceding our arrival at Block 23 G, Trifonov residence.

At this point, the girl was nervously chatting away about random things, about a song she liked and the weather while trying to comb her hair with her fingers. This was the first chance I had to actually look at her so I closed my

150

mouth and watched the girl talk, sweating with anticipation. I wasn't expecting anything good.

Underneath the dirt, her face was unusually pale for a Romani girl. She was about thirteen or so, with partially henna-dyed light brown hair and green eyes that hadn't seen much sleep in the last year or so. Despite all the loud cursing, the bruises and the overall state of her, I honestly thought that she was quite beautiful.

Mom didn't say much at first. She moved around the kitchen, sorting out pans and dishes, making clicking sounds with her tongue. I don't know why mothers always make these clicking sounds when they are utterly disappointed but they always do. It's a thing.

After doing the tongue-clicking thing for a while, she placed a bowl of chicken soup and a cup of coffee in front of the girl. I was ordered to get my own and D didn't get any.

Mom watched the girl eat for a minute, pointed to the dress she was wearing and said that it looked 'a little familiar'. The dress did look familiar. Was it one of Mom's? In that case, I must have forgotten that I took it.

While the girl was devouring her soup and slurping her coffee loudly, Mom began to do this thing she does – that same thing that her mother did so well – patching people up. And she did it with incredible finesse.

She asked about the girl's age and background while refilling the bowl and the coffee cup for the second time. She didn't poke or probe, just explained to her that 'it was natural to know these things because mothers must know such things'. She made it very clear that luxuries such as bowls of soup, the promise of a hot bath, and the attention of a loving mother, were only reserved for her own children, the girl being one of them all of a sudden. She exaggerated massively, but I wasn't allowed to point that out. Whenever I opened my mouth to tell my side of the story, Mom looked at me sternly, told me to shut up and focussed on the girl.

The girl talked for about an hour. She told us stories about her life that were only held together by some kind of invisible thread that had something to do with sex in an ocean of events that could impossibly fit within a thirteen-year timeline. She ended every story with a sigh and 'this is why I can never return to my family'.

Most of the stories were designed to fit that same message – that she would never return to 'a family who ALWAYS forces me to do things that I don't want to do'. She didn't see herself as being homeless but rather 'on the road'. In Plovdiv, she was 'free to fuck whomever she wanted' and she didn't care much if she lived or died 'as long as she was fucked by real men'.

I kept thinking of my long-lost classmate Eime in desperate attempts to remember if I saw any pregnant bellies in the mixture of morbid smiles, pubic hair, skin and erections that day. I wasn't sure.

Mom reacted to every one of the girl's stories with surprisingly understanding nods while firing questions at her in the otherwise seemingly mundane everyday talk about 'life in the city' versus 'life in the village'. After several long hours of endless stories about the city, the girl's village, mothers, lovers, 'real men' and their genitals, we put the girl on a bus home to her own mother.

I still don't know how Mom did it, but there we were.

Much to my dismay and disappointment, the girl was not only fed, washed and cleaned but also awarded some of my clothes. She departed with a heart full of nostalgia for her home and family and pockets full of coins. Mom must've put all of our money there given the girl's departure was preceded by a very invasive, if I may say so, raid of the entire flat and our own pockets, including D's. No questions asked and permissions given.

That evening, I took the bus to my room in the attic, dragged everything out of the place, burned the sheets, locked the door, tossed the key underneath the doormat and left.

I never saw that room again.

Needless to say, the whole 'broken Romani girl debacle' left a nasty taste in my mouth. D tried to smooth things over with me, but I didn't feel safe with her anymore. T hated being caught in the middle so he tried to smooth things over too. In my eyes, that made him an accomplice.

There was also the pressure to always meet at D's. I wanted to spend time with my friends, but there were parents, a toddler and zero musical instruments at mine so meeting there was out of the question. I started spending my tiny allowance on things like cinema tickets and backstage passes just so I could see my friends before they headed off to D's. When my money ran out, I stayed at home waiting for T to come to me, which he gladly did. He took this boyfriend and girlfriend business very seriously.

It wasn't long before my dad and my boyfriend were spending several nights a week together, watching TV, reminiscing about their days in the military and drinking beer saying 'cheers' and 'to your health, young man' TO EACH OTHER. It was like dating my father, which to a 17-year-old is as attractive as dating a dead rat.

I watched them smile, embrace and laugh out loud at the most juvenile jokes that my father could possibly muster. Mom occupied herself with the usual chores: mixing things in big plastic bowls, shoving trays in the oven and taking them out twenty minutes later, or watching over the slow-cooking rice dish that always made better leftovers than the best pizza.

Little did I know that I would spend a lifetime trying to replace them with other people in distant places, people with seemingly more knowledge of the world but none of the empathy and courage that I grew up with. Little did I know that I would make love and whisper things in other languages, in the ears of men that knew nothing of death, broken souls, poverty, despair or sacrifice. I knew nothing of all that. Evening after evening, I would sit there watching these two faulty men telling each other jokes that didn't seem funny at all, wishing for other people and other things.

One night, just as I was sitting there watching Dad and T celebrate their relationship again, I started thinking that it might be time to say goodbye to D and the rest of my attic circle. The noisy TV program blasting from Dad's improvised speakers was fading into the type of 'popular' music that was usually played at half-empty state-run department stores five minutes before closing time. It was that moment of the evening, thirty minutes or so before midnight, when the national anthem marked the ending of all programs for the day and my parents suddenly remembered that I was sitting there in the room with them. And voila, as if they were following a manuscript, all faces turned to me, eyes started blinking and a familiar question echoed: "How is your art going, kid?"

I was just about to fire a myriad of cynical answers at them when my sister entered the living room riding on a small plastic toy car and honked her horn with delight. I sighed with relief thinking 'phew, I'm off the hook', picked her up and started braiding her shiny newly washed hair. Mom put down her fork and watched the two of us cuddling.

It wasn't long before T felt left out. He stretched his arms and offered Dari a ride on his shoulders. She wasn't up to it. My hugs and the absence of Russian TV blasting out fake pompous laughter, an always annoying and never laugh-inducing companion of propaganda sketches, had made her sleepy. She leaned her little head on my shoulder and asked to go to bed. I picked her up, walked down the hallway to our room and put her down in her bed. She wouldn't let me leave so I sat down on the floor and rested my head on the corner of her pillow pretending to snore. She closed her eyes and fell asleep with a smile.

I woke up an hour or so later realising that I had fallen asleep on her tiny bed and rolled over to a bedside table with a pillow under my arm, which was an utterly useless place for a pillow. T had left, and Mom was sleeping, but Dad was still up listening to the white noise from a small transistor radio. *He is at it again*, I thought, feeling happy that my father was returning to the things that he used to do before Troj's death, like listening to the glitchy Radio Free Europe hiding in the kitchen. I walked in, still clutching Dari's small embroidered pillow and asked if I could sit there with him for a while. He turned to me and smiled.

"Sure...come in! Sit! I can't get anything out of this radio anyway."
"Why aren't you sleeping?"

Dad didn't answer. He took off his glasses, wiped the lenses carefully with his cotton vest, put them back on and stared at me with anticipation.

"You didn't answer my question."
"Didn't I? What question was that?"
"Your art...how is that going? Your boyfriend told me that you went to see a famous artist and showed him your portfolio. I can't believe that I had to hear it from him and not from you."

I didn't know what to tell him, the part where I went to a luxurious studio in a penthouse with a terrace overlooking the town centre, sat opposite a fat old bearded man hoping to get some valuable advice on my work, was offered wine which I drunk out of politeness, felt dizzy within minutes and had to fight off the old pervert until he was too tired of grouping me by my breasts and genitals; or the part where, disappointed by not being able to pin me down to the bed, probably due to poor health, he sat up, opened my portfolio and said that I 'had something but was too negligent of my potential and too unaware of what a person like him could do for my budding womanhood or artistic career'.

"I didn't tell you because it wasn't much to tell really. The guy said that I had potential, but you know…was lacking the right connections or something. I'm not sure what he meant."

I lied. I knew exactly what he meant. Just before I zipped my trousers up and ran for the door, I heard him say that 'Manasi wasn't the right man for me'. I had managed to get him off me by pretending to be sick and forcing myself to throw up in his bathroom, making sure he heard every sound, including the coughing and the splashing of sour wine down the toilet. He must have understood that I wasn't going to do anything for him that day so he fired his last bullet and somehow that statement about Manasi was it. I ran down the stairs shaking and crying because hearing that last statement hurt more than the humiliation, the violence and the fear put together. These fat pathetic old men were ROTATING us. When one of us was 'picked' by one of them, her fate was sealed forever and there was nowhere to run.

In anticipation of more answers from me, Dad closed his eyes and started drawing shapes with his fingers in the air.

"I like your drawings of that woman with the airplane. Beautiful composition. And you seem to know your planes. Did I teach you that?"

"Yes, you did, you old soldier you."

I sat opposite him smiling and feeling relaxed for the first time in months. It was nice.

24

I grew tired of T. It was sad because he did everything he could to make me smile. He calmed me down with sweet talk and hugs when I was angry, and he always knew to kiss the soft line between my legs leading to the bulge underneath my belly whenever I didn't pay attention while making love. He was never angry and always kind. But it didn't matter what he did or said. There was this one all important thing that he didn't know how to do and it became a dealbreaker. He didn't know how to make me feel safe.

I'm not even sure that he understood how much I needed to feel safe and how little I knew about the double-sided nature of need. He was just the first of many who didn't see that urgent call for safety underneath the smiles, care and constant validation that I've always been really good at giving. They all breathed in and exhaled that love and care until they realised that something was very wrong. Then they started longing, often greedily, for more of the same but without the strange unsettling need lurking underneath. That was something I couldn't give because it didn't exist.

T had the same name as my father's. It was a coincidence that I thought showcased irony at its best. But I was being naive and unfair. That name of his broke more than one layer of thick ice. After several painful years of wondering if I liked boys or, God forbid, girls, or if I was maybe destined to end up a childless spinster because of my picky ways and restless nature, my parents rejoiced at the prospect of this boy who not only was a talented musician but also had 'father's great name'. He was introduced to the family and immediately accepted as 'The Namesake'.

I didn't mean to be cruel to him. I knew that many of the things I did were things any teenage girl would consider doing or do without hesitation, and yet I wished to apologise. I never did apologise though. To this day, I wonder if Troj and what happened to him had given me the wrong idea about what I could and couldn't do to people who loved me. After all, I was the sister of 'that boy' and as such I was allowed to be lost, inconsistent and even cruel sometimes.

Although I would happily trade any privileges for one last look at Troj's smiling living face, feeling untouchable felt sort of like a little bit of clemency.

Until, it didn't.

I am certain that my relationship with T would have ended sooner if it wasn't for the constant art practice trips and communist camps that we were marched to, whenever possible. Being in different cities meant we were 'on hold' and breaking up was delayed for the unforeseeable future. That year was going to be my last school year. Most of the kids in my class would eventually hit the schools, shops and factory floors and leave all things Art behind. Only a few chosen ones would continue their education at the one and only Sofia Art Academy. And because there wasn't much time left to shape us, T.L. Art School decided to send us to military camp.

This wasn't a regular military camp but a special camp designed for the children of communist Intelligentsia, meaning everyone above the age of seventeen was there to torment us, abuse us, laugh at us and scare us. It was hot beyond anyone's concept of hot, 40–45 degrees Celsius or so. The fact that the camp was in the middle of the woods didn't do much to improve the desert-like conditions, possibly due to Komsomol leaders finding all sorts of excuses to march us to the open fields to bake under the scorching sun.

When I left for the camp with Rosie and a couple of other girls from the School of English and Mathematics, I was expecting good times and none of the torture. A month away from T and my family sounded pretty good right about then. I thought that I was going to have a nice camp experience with the occasional flirt, late night girl-talk, giggles and plenty of adventure. Instead, I was presented with two options: either do exactly as I was told while fooling myself into enjoying the experience (by gaining some muscle and learning how to take apart a Kalashnikov rifle in eight seconds for example), or hate my life wallowing in self-pity. I chose the latter option.

The days at military camp were long. We were woken up as early as 5:30 am and ordered to run around the barracks. Breakfast was at 7 so we had some time to wash up and dress ourselves in stinky military gear. Then we would line up for marching and field exercises. The all too familiar practice of lining up after my breasts was once again introduced, this time by a balding Komsomol leader who saw himself as some kind of comical genius. I bit my tongue because the outcomes of reactions verbalised, or in any other way expressed, were too unpredictable to take any chances. We were half-dead by noon so we were given lunch and the chance to get some much-needed afternoon rest. But afternoon naps were close to impossible to get because we were constantly told to do chores for the Komsomol leaders and other people eighteen or older, from washing their underwear to cleaning their private quarters and meeting rooms.

It took them about five miserable days to erase our identities. We ceased to be artists, musicians, mathematicians or polyglots and became just girls ready to be broken and moulded into 'the secondary citizens' we were 'born to be'.

Just as I was getting the hang of it, after the first week or so, I realised that the torment had just begun. Some of the old Komsomol leaders left and a couple of younger men came to replace them. These new guards were far worse than the previous batch. They were vicious and greedy for much more than just the occasional serving of snacks, washing and cleaning. They didn't lurk around and flirt but walked straight to us and took whatever they wanted.

This was unexpected and highly dangerous so Rosie and I had to do something. First, we switched trousers. Then we threw away our makeup and stopped washing our hair and armpits. We made sure that we were unattractive but were cautious to not overdo it because that would have been dangerous too. Our new strategy didn't help the bullying but minimised the heavy petting down to one or two failed attempts per day, which at that point was the best we could possibly hope for.

Our new tactic bought us no more than two days of healthy distance. One of the new guards started making comments about my looks so I had to start washing my hair again. Also, we were issued new uniform trousers that we damaged only slightly, but that backfired. We were ordered to mend everyone else's trousers 'as punishment for not respecting the uniform'.

While not respecting the uniform was considered an offence too silly to be officially punishable, it was made clear to us that by 'altering our looks' we had opened a whole new can of worms, and make no mistake, the shenanigans were coming for us, that we knew for sure. How did we know? Well, the fact that Rosie and I were made to spend considerable time using our hands (which was something that we obviously found quite enjoyable), sheltered in the cool shade of the main washroom barrack while every single person our age was running in the sun sweating like a mountain lizard and cursing through her teeth in a gas mask that had been around the face of a unwashed teen just over one thousand times…that fact was a dead giveaway that they were coming for us as soon as all the clothes were mended. So, naturally, we took our time.

We were left alone for the best part of the afternoon on the first day of mending duty. It was funny to us and 'so typical of men' that we were ordered to do this. Forcing us to do something that men hated doing and thinking that it would be a great punishment for us…that was just plain silly. Rosie and I spent most of the time making jokes and telling each other stories about the many failures of man-kind. We 'knew nothing about such things' we were told time and time again. How could we ever imagine the burdens of men trying to be the best that Communism had to offer? Isn't it utterly comprehensible that men with such burdens may 'deserve' a bit of liberty now and then even if it is at someone else's expense? Besides, it is very much okay if that someone is weaker. Right? Weakness is a punishable thing. Isn't it so?

And that, ladies and gents, is where comedy resides. It hides in the cracks between weakness and entitlement; it is ridiculously surprising and marvellous when you see it manifest with your own eyes and, on that day, it was wet and wearing thick coke bottle bottom glasses with a piece of tape over one eye.

Ah, the humanity!

Galja, although I didn't know her name at the time, was a math protege and a remarkable chess player. Apart from your entire family being dismantled and your siblings sent to an orphanage on another mountain that wasn't part of your realm of mountains, being sent to military camp must have been the worst thing that could possibly happen to a girl like Galja. She tried to be patient, bless her, to the point where she would twitch and yet keep silent. For someone blessed with total unawareness regarding the privilege that comes with reasonably good looks, I was left speechless at the reality of her existence and, most importantly, the way she managed to patiently 'handle it'.

On the second day of our 'punishment', we were relocated to one of the barracks closest to the Komsomol leadership quarters. That was ominous to say the least. It had to be a prelude to something awful, we thought and sat quietly eavesdropping on the leadership while sweating and shivering with unwelcomed anticipation.

They were playing chess in the cooler part of the barrack, under the stairs to the kitchen floor, sipping chilled beer and only occasionally looking through the window to check on the running female youth just to make sure nobody died between then and ten minutes prior. "We have a chess girl in the camp, you know…" one of them said with a sigh following a loudly discussed loss at two previous matches. Boy, those folks were dumb. How can you possibly fit three

159

chess matches in one hour? Why are they even trying? Get yourselves a dart set or something…Damn! There was a blessing there though. At least, they kept themselves busy.

Galja was called into the room and ordered 'to state her case'. "What? Huh?" she muttered and started twitching again. The main Komsomol guy, the one that saw himself as some kind of comedic genius, found her twitching very amusing. He sat for a while summoning said comedic genius and thinking of something 'amusing' to say. We moved our positions closer to the open (praise the Lord) door and awaited the amusing thing fearing total nastiness while being thankful that it wasn't us this particular time.

"Look at you, private! You are not fit to be here. In fact, I'm dismissing you altogether. You are to be reprimanded and sentenced to confinement for the rest of the camp."

Galja's face turned white as a bleached uniform collar.

"Why? Wh…at have I done? I was just…" she mumbled. The twitching stopped and her eyes filled with tears (we didn't really see her tears due to darkness in the shade of the stairs, but it definitely sounded like she was crying).

"You are clearly an ALIEN. By Lenin, look at yas…I have no other choice but to stop your spying ways. I have to lock you up in order to keep you from reporting back to the mothership."

He looked mighty proud of what he thought was a very funny prank. His cronies didn't disappoint. Their drunken laughter echoed in the barracks for a while, bouncing back and forth between the rusty lockers.

Rosie and I were stunned. We were usually pretty good at guessing the outcomes of such events. After all, those Komsomol dummies were quite predictable. But this time, we had no clue what was coming. Was she going to finally break and fall apart? Was she going to admit defeat and call her parents thus providing entertainment where, according to the unwritten laws of Komsomol, entertainment was due? At that point, all scenarios were possible.

Well, one thing was for sure…we greatly underestimated her beautiful brain. Suddenly, Galja grinned with her mouth wide open to show all her teeth including the budding wisdom teeth in the back and stamped loudly with her boot, took her sweaty uniform jacket off and turned around towards us. She looked bewildered for a second then smiled, winked, walked past me and Rosie, stopped in front of one of the lockers and started hitting it with her fists.

"Mothership, come in! Come in, Mothership! They are on to me. Abort! Abort! Those village whores you planned to use tonight to lure them in and conduct medical experiments on them…maybe better to postpone until the coast is clear."

Somehow she knew that 'village whores' were coming that night. She used her knowledge well. She wasn't allowed anywhere near the leadership after that. That was a blessing beyond all blessings.

The end of military camp was weeks away, and just as we had lost all hope, the chief officer in charge of military education in the area came to inspect 'the troops'. The rough treatment stopped for a while, and we were given some much-needed time to rest and visit the nearby village.

It was more of a small mountain town than a village. The place seemed really pleasant at first, but as soon as we entered the centre, we knew that this wasn't just any town. It was segregated, with Roma families living in the outskirts in misery, the communist upper class occupying the centre and regular folks between them and the Roma neighbourhoods. We saw many men in uniforms and several women wearing the typical army secretary attire: heavily bleached white blouses, scarves and petrol-green pencil-skirts. There was a theatre, two cinemas, several entertainment centres, pubs and a disco. It was clear that the small town was built to maintain a large military complex. There had to be a hidden one somewhere up the hill, we thought, but didn't see any. It was very well hidden indeed.

We returned from our walk through town surprisingly refreshed. We had bought snacks that we shared with the other campers. After that, Rosie and I went on a hunt for privacy, preferably somewhere in the bushes. Not being able to draw and paint for weeks at a time felt worse than not washing properly. We walked around the camp until we found the ideal spot for some much-needed conversation and drawing. It was underneath the kitchen stairs and had three concrete walls and an opening on the left side. There was no door, but somebody had parked their car just in front of it. It was perfect.

We fell asleep and missed the evening count.

Our absence caused a bit of a stir. We heard the calls and were quick to sneak out and crawl to our beds, but pretending that we were there all along and the whole thing was 'just a misunderstanding' didn't work. We were ordered to report to the chief military officer in the morning to receive our punishment.

It turned out that the officer was an acquaintance of Rosie's parents. He took one look at the two of us and recognised me immediately. "Aha," he said with a smirk and pointed at me. "You are that girl," he said. I didn't know what else to do but nod in agreement.

The punishment was a night of no sleep guarding the camp entrance. It didn't matter, we were too edgy and exhausted to sleep anyway. We just stood there waiting for "village whores" to walk by so we can tell them about Galja's mothership.

25

It was T who unknowingly introduced me to the person who would take me away from him and change my fate unwillingly and forever.

T wouldn't stop talking about a Swedish man, 'an old army friend', that was soon coming to visit. This man was not a real Swede but the son of high-ranked military people, possibly secret service, who worked at the embassy in Stockholm. Their actual jobs were well camouflaged behind titles like 'transport attaché' and 'trade liaison' so nobody knew exactly what they did at the embassy. T's friend was very intellectual, I was told, and quite the 'pencil-enthusiast'. I wasn't sure if that meant that he was a writer or maybe an artist. I asked around and was told that he was 'both'.

A month or so after first hearing about 'The Swede', another one of T's friends, the kind and generous N, invited us to a late night party at his villa. It was quite obvious that N's parents had money. He lived in a large house in the outskirts of Plovdiv, all clad in marble with gold-plated details everywhere. The driveway had a Mercedes logo cast in its concrete floor and a matching brand new Mercedes car parked by, with flowerbeds and a fountain around it. N's home was embellished to the point of unmistakable kitsch which I found quite entertaining.

I didn't feel like drinking so I ended up watching everyone else get drunk. I had returned from military camp with a nasty cold and knew that if I overdid it with the drinks and smokes I'd be leaving that posh villa in an ambulance.

It was almost midnight when we arrived at the house. T had given up on his friend at that point despite numerous phone calls and reassurances. But the phone rang at about 1 am and five minutes later, there he was, getting off a town car carrying gifts. He had fancy cigarettes, cassette tapes and a vinyl record for T. It was *Quadrophenia* by The Who.

That's how I met Ilya.

The night was less adventurous than T anticipated. They were all drunk already and 'The Swede' tried his best to catch up. An hour or so into the night, my boyfriend collapsed on a couch half-conscious and fell asleep soon after.

Looking for a night breeze somewhere quiet, I sat by a window next to the balcony and just people-watched for a while.

Ilya stared at me throughout the party. Whether I looked at a particular person, eavesdropping or browsed in one of the foreign magazines lying around, the moment I looked up at him, he would be staring. It wasn't unpleasant, just awkward considering T had just passed out on the couch.

I don't know if what happened afterwards can be called chemistry, attraction or just two people taking a chance against their better judgement. I am not even sure if I remember everything as it happened. Memories were most certainly scrambled and rather twisted by what happened afterwards. The one thing I recall is a long conversation about books we had read, liked and disliked. Then there was a kiss. I remember the taste, the awkward feeling throughout the twenty seconds of it and the fact that he started to giggle shortly after, which left me wishing for a do-over of that entire night.

I tried to forget about the kiss and all its awkwardness, but I couldn't. I had to break up with T for sure. Somehow, I thought that the best way to do that would be to cut him off completely. I am so ashamed to admit that I never thought of the hurt I was causing. And even more at odds with my character, I seriously considered him deserving of what was done to him. By me.

I wasn't longing for Ilya in any way, but there was something in him that fascinated me. There was something underneath his expensive sweater, thin glasses and unruly but well thought out hair that whispered of many contradictions and even a hint of deception. That little bit of mystery sent my teenage imagination spinning. I could also tell that he was very smart and well-read, which has always made me weak in the knees.

Weeks and months went by. School was entering its final phase. All of my classmates were working on their final annual exhibition foolishly believing in its life-changing powers. I was bored by it and didn't feel any excitement about the work I was doing. It was a lie, all of it. It was so much a lie that I don't remember what the paintings looked like. The teachers warned me about 'not living up to my potential', but I paid very little attention to them thinking, *Yeah, I know what that means, you filthy old perverts.*

Thoughts of Ilya crossed my mind rarely as I was enjoying a brand new romantic adventure that for the first time featured a boy exactly my age. We spent most of our time chatting away about mundane things, laughing, kissing and touching each other. He liked me in a simple and comforting kind of way.

Together, we decided that we didn't have any artistic career potential so making mediocre art was fine 'as long as life made sense'. The plan was to become art teachers.

Everything about this boy felt…safe.

And just like that, I received a postcard.

It created quite a stir around the block. 'A postcard from Sweden' was something well worth anyone's envy. And there was a letter after that. A letter was a thing sealed in secrecy. Although bragged about, the content of that letter was only mentioned with hesitation and never revealed to people outside our immediate family. Dad didn't trust Ilya at all. Needless to say, he missed his namesake and the idea of marrying me away to a talented handsome young man who could hold his drink and joke on the same profanity level, appealed to him.

Mom, on the other hand, was being superstitious. She seemed to think that something like this could be easily taken away, either through the kind of black magic people like Eunice were capable of, or by someone who was either prettier than I was or more suitable to become the wife of a communist prince like Ilya. She was shaking in her boots with fear. I was appalled by her behavior thinking that she couldn't wait to get rid of me and marry me off. I wished it all gone: love letters, final exams, mediocre art and nosey neighbours obsessing with all things Sweden. I decided to take a trip to the mountains. Grandma was long gone, but I had a friend who lived in a town not too far from the Sakar Mountains. *Close enough*, I thought and made plans.

One early morning in April, I sneaked into the living room, removed the letter from its place in the spotlight right underneath Troj's picture and next to the Romanian porcelain tea set that Mom polished every week, tucked it away in a drawer and started packing. I took some underwear, two t-shirts, a sweater and a book, shoved them into a brown leather bag and headed for the door. For some reason, just before leaving, I decided to return to the said drawer. I dug up the letter, scribbled the telephone number underneath Ilya's neat 'Sincerely Yours' on a piece of paper and dropped it in my bag. I had a premonition of some kind and I didn't know what it meant.

Stoyan was a puppet maker. He used to work at the Marionette Theatre in Plovdiv but moved back to his hometown Sliven in a rush. It might have had something to do with me, but I shouldn't give myself too much credit for the life-changing decisions of other people.

We had a short encounter right before the whole Manasi ordeal happened. My short-lived relationship with him was so outside my family circle, my home, life and history that it became one of those short romances that linger in the air for a little bit, gets neglected and ends without closure. I even told Manasi about it. A week or so before he carried me up the stairs to the loft for the first time, he asked me if I had a boyfriend. I mentioned Stoyan and added that I liked him a lot and thought that he would make 'a very good first'. Manasi disapproved loudly. He explained to me that 'boys rarely made good firsts'.

That April day, I decided to get my closure once and for all. I took the bus to Sliven and found Stoyan in the local Marionette theatre making puppets.

He seemed genuinely happy and pleasantly surprised to see me, but there was a hint of hesitation in the way he behaved. I didn't blame him. I had become more of an acquaintance than a friend. The girl he knew was insecure and fearful but also insanely curious and creative. The young woman he met at the door that day appeared to have plenty of strong opinions but not much else. I was cautiously rationing my empathy at that moment in my life.

I stayed there for a while. Stoyan lived in a cosy room in the attic of an old townhouse in the centre of Sliven, and the theatre where he worked making marionette dolls was a quick walk away from his home. He should have told me to call my mother and head back home. Instead, he washed my clothes, made sure I had enough sleep, coffee and food and tended to my every need. He introduced me to many of his friends just so that I wouldn't be alone when he was at work.

The people I met there resembled characters in a pre-revolution Russian novel. They wore wool suits, knitted polo sweaters and checkered caps with metal pins matching the pins on their lapels. Everything they said sounded dramatic, clever and sometimes quite sweet. There was only one girl in the group. She was strikingly beautiful and always dressed lavishly in faux furs, short leather skirts and colorful blouses adorned with bows and brooches. Stoyan treated her in the same way he treated me, with utmost attention and care. "She really needs it," he would say. "She lays with everybody who pays attention to her, and when I ask her why she does it, she says it was because THEY wanted to." He would shake his head disapprovingly and continue tending to my every need.

There was also a filmmaker who had lost the use of his left leg and arm after a diving accident. He 'harpooned himself in the sea', I was told. I couldn't tell if they were making fun of him or telling the truth. To me, he looked like somebody who had recently suffered a severe stroke. But what did I know? Nothing, I suppose. He couldn't walk without his cane and made sure everybody knew that he hated 'the stupid stick'.

The more I got to know 'The Filmmaker', the more he reminded me of one of my father's drinking buddies, a tall and skinny man that everyone referred to as 'The Doctor'. Said 'Doctor' was bitter and angry simply because he was aging. His body had lost its beauty and women didn't pay attention to him anymore. Back in the days, he was known as a charmer, a 'wide boy' of a sort.

There was also a quiet young man who said very little but took notes everywhere he went. Just as The Filmmaker, he dressed in clothes fit for a proletariat revolutionary, from the pointy worn-out shoes to the grandpa cap.

The end of the week was rapidly approaching. There were nine days left of my spring vacation, and I didn't really know what to do and where to go. When The Filmmaker and the young faux fur clad woman suggested a trip up the mountain, I asked if I could join them. Stoyan was growing restless and irritable which I took as a sign that I had outstayed my welcome. I gathered my things, thanked him for everything and kissed him on the cheek. He nodded and whispered a shy 'Stay in touch'.

We were picked up in a beat-up old Russian Lada, the kind that wouldn't survive a trip up a very small hill, let alone tackle the mighty Balkan, but I was willing to give it a chance.

Driving up a mountain in Bulgaria is like ascending to heaven, unless you are trapped in an old Russian car full of people who equate seatbelts to crutches and sing Vysotskij songs (very badly, I should add) while smoking filterless cigarettes. I closed my eyes and waited for the trip to end. And apart from the occasional elbow in my ribs and loud whispering in my ear now and again, they let me be.

I wish I could remember that ride up the Balkan Mountain above Sliven. I haven't been there since and could use an image or two. It's said to be breathtakingly beautiful. But because I had my eyes closed, all memories from that day in April have been replaced with images from other trips many years later. What can I say…my brain does this a lot, fills in the gaps and refuses all things linear.

Rodopa is the mountain that makes Plovdiv a pressure cooker in the summer as it surrounds the city like the walls of a saucepan. The higher up one goes, the cooler and greener it gets. I remember this one particular trip up the mountains there. It's the only time I had been anywhere with Dad's Aunt Tochka and her husband.

Dad wanted to share the mountain with his grandchildren and maybe even take us all fishing. My daughter Saga was about four years old. She insisted on sitting in her big brother's lap and kept her distance from everyone else. I didn't force her to hug relatives or bow to her elders as one was expected to do in Bulgaria. Some of these people were quite frightening. Dad's uncle, for example. He never slept, had only one eye and looked like a very old man although he was in his early sixties at that point.

The scariest of relatives, Eunice, was a walking dictionary on how to weaponise existence so she insisted on having ridiculous fits over mundane things while giving advice on how my children should be disciplined. My cousins were mostly kind but kept getting a little too close and touchy-feely, always kissing and squeezing, My children hated that.

It was supposed to be just us and Mom and Dad, but it was somehow decided that all available relatives still able to walk, would join us in a second, slightly overcrowded unidentifiable Russian vehicle (It might have been an old Moskvitch crossed with an even older Volga. My relatives are handy like that).

The kids and I were sitting in the backseat of our car. Dad was driving with Mom sitting next to him, doing her superstitious crosses in the air and mumbling. The second car was also full, although there were only four people sitting in it.

'Tochka' was the one-eyed uncle's wife. 'Tochka' means 'dot' in Bulgarian. The nickname was my son's fault. Her actual name was Totka, but he happened to pronounce it wrong once and the name stuck because of how round she was. She occupied the back seat squeezing the air out of her husband. Their son was driving and my sister was sitting in the front seat next to him. Tochka's son was Dad's cousin and another namesake of his (I know what you are thinking and the answer is NO, not all men in my family have the same name. That would be too confusing).

We stopped not one, not two, but three times. Once for a bathroom break and two times for the traditional family picnics. We would choose a spot close to a river or a spring and park the cars by the road. Blankets would be laid down to make a large table and the canvas Dad used to cover the car would serve as both a ceiling and a floor in an improvised tent. Then Tochka would sit down in the centre and Mom would serve an enormous smorgasbord of traditional dishes she'd prepared for the occasion. There was tsatsiki, imam bayildi, banitsa pastry with feta cheese and spinach and lots of rice dishes made with lamb, aubergines, peppers and tomatoes. There were also pickles of all imaginable sorts.

Our last and highest goal, both physically and spiritually, was of course Rodopa's infamous jem – the Bachkovo Monastery. We took our time to enjoy…I want to say 'nature' but I can only remember the unimaginable abundance of food.

I have a special relationship with this particular monastery. When the Berlin Wall fell and it became possible for me to travel back to Bulgaria, I went back to be baptised there. It wasn't something I had planned.

After enduring a horrific flight to Sofia, being stopped and frisked at the border numerous times, reduced to tears and made to pay a hefty bribe to end the threats, poking and probing, my son and I took the train to the vineyard where Ivanka lived alone in the old family home. It was just a big stone house with some land attached to it at that point. The vines were there, but nobody made wine. There I was, sitting next to Tochka, trying to persuade her to reconsider writing a return address on a package of hand-knitted socks she had made for the ex-communist leader Todor Zivkov so that 'he wouldn't freeze in jail'. She wrote the address anyway and sent it off smiling.

That night, we ended up discussing politics and that heated discussion resulted in an outright war over religion and the fact that Dad didn't believe in any higher power. Mom did what she always did – sat pouting and staring at Dad sternly with her arms crossed on her chest (she would even walk with her arms crossed and only uncross them when we weren't looking). I tried to explain to them all that there was a difference between religion and spirituality but was gravely misunderstood and ended up threatening to 'climb to Bachkovo and get baptised'. Dad dared me, and there I was, climbing Rodopa for the first time since our ski trips in secondary school.

Baptism rituals at Bachkovo were carried out in the old church below the monks' quarters. It was a very small church, but it had the spiritual patina to inspire faith in anyone who entered through its narrow doors.

The old church building was unlike any other church I had ever seen, Bulgarian or foreign. It looked like something that emerged from the ground after an earthquake. It consisted of several smaller buildings that met in all sorts of strange ways and formed something that looked like an organic mass rather than a temple. One room led to another, which led to a third and a fourth until we didn't know what was what. The aisles were lower and narrower towards the middle, but other than that, the rooms were similarly dark with paint everywhere. Each small surface was covered with paintings that told centuries old stories about everything from unhappy loves to hell fires. Whoever painted these walls must have been obsessed with fires. There were depictions of hell fires and bonfires scattered around the church grounds with the occasional image of full-on Hell featuring many firepits with demons flying around. For some unknown to me reason, there were no souls in those firepits, only burning books and scrolls.

The exterior of the church was also covered with paintings and there were mounted photos of famous icons from the region. Dad and I looked at them while we waited in line to register. We laughed at all the painted men who wrote books and played instruments while being showered with flowers by cherubs and angels flying above their heads. The painted men were all fully clothed. Then we looked at the painted women who ran around naked with demons chasing them and beating them with sticks and nettles, in their separate Hell on the other side. We laughed uncontrollably at that point despite some very cold stares from representatives of the clergy. "The painter was madly in love with a beautiful woman from Plovdiv, but the feeling wasn't mutual," we were informed.

The clergy let in all women and children but the men were ordered to remain outside. The church was too small and 'they had to compromise'. My father protested loudly to no effect. Mom's sister Dora had arrived so she was asked to be my godmother. She was a spiritual person so she accepted with delight. We stood in the queue and waited while Mom tried to silence my little sister with candy from her bottomless bag.

About twenty infants and small children were baptised before my baptism took place. The oldest girl was no older than four. She was baptised just before I was, kicking and screaming. Clothes and socks flew everywhere and her mother had to physically push her into the murky holy water so that the priest could say his 'Amen' and the rest. She was still sobbing when I was asked to step forward.

The priest took a short break to regroup before he performed my baptism ceremony. Typically, each child would be held by the priest and dipped in the baptismal bowl naked, but you couldn't do that with a grown woman so he placed a smaller bowl on the ground in front of me and bathed my feet.

It took me a while before I had the courage to look up. The priest was younger than me. That shocked me so I forgot what I was doing and the ceremony came to a halt. Suddenly, I heard a scream and the still weeping four-year-old girl landed in front of me waving her thin little arms. "Why aren't moms made to strip naked?" she screamed.

"Because then everyone would want to become a priest," my dad shouted from the crowded entrance. The crowd roared with laughter.

It took a long while before the priest could resume his ceremony.

I made a pact with Bachkovo that day. I would keep visiting as long as it kept its history unblemished by greed and damaged by tourists seeking blessings they rarely deserved.

This was my second trip to the monastery with the kids. We had to wait for Tochka more than once. She was huffing and puffing up the hill and then down the hill while her husband held her hand trying not to drag her. If he ever dared to attempt dragging her, she would have hit him with her version of Mom's bottomless purse.

I got impatient with them two, grabbed Saga's hand and started walking around the familiar grounds. To the left of the entrance, we saw a garden and to the right we saw the water fountain that everyone always flocked around. The water in the well was said to be blessed so people came from all over the land to fill their containers. In the past, there would have been beautiful glass bottles decorated with crocheted nylon creations. Nowadays, it was mostly plastic containers and empty Fanta bottles.

When Tochka finally emerged from the crowded exit, a brawl had broken out at the well. The cause of the brawl was well visible in the middle of the crowd – a sweaty middle-aged man with a large belly holding about a dozen plastic bottles in his hands, one between each finger. The fight seemed to be about his belly taking too much space. His loudest opponent looked like an older version of Tochka but sounded more like if Eunice and the Bearded Lady had a baby and the baby was really old and bitter.

The fight ended as suddenly as it started. A shiny new Mercedes bus had just pulled up by the well. The crowd abandoned their disputes and flocked to inspect the unusual vehicle. The bus door opened and a dark-skinned man in a short-sleeve uniform rushed out, sat under a tree and impatiently lit a cigarette. A couple of blond heads could be seen peeking through the door.

It took Saga exactly three seconds to recognise the typical Swedish tourist on a summer holiday type. She started pulling my dress saying, "Swedes! Swedes!" I took her hand, and we walked up to the Swedes who were starting to gather at the first market stand outside the monastery. Every single one of them wore a white t-shirt, a beige pair of shorts, white tube socks and sandals. That was probably why the crowd at the well, including the vicious Tochka copy and Big Belly, couldn't stop looking. The Tochka copy shook her head and concluded that 'it must be Germans'. The others nodded in agreement because evidently 'Germans liked uniforms' and the crowd around the well dispersed.

Saga and I approached the Swedes to help them with their souvenir shopping. Saga walked up to a woman with glasses, showed her a hand-painted blue ceramic tortoise and explained (in fluent Swedish) that 'she could play music on it by pressing her fingers against the tiny holes on its back'. The woman looked at the beautiful odd instrument, showed it to her husband and patiently waited for his response. He waved his hand as to say that he wasn't interested, turned around and started walking towards the beer stand. The woman put the tortoise back on the table, apologised shyly and walked away from Saga as fast as she possibly could. Saga didn't care much. She had decided that she absolutely had to have a musical instrument and the only way she could have one was for me to buy it for her at double the price because 'whoever made it worked really hard and it was beautiful'.

For the most part, I struggled to understand why these talented hard-working women charged so little for things that took so long to shape, burn and paint so I shrugged, smiled at Saga and bought three of them, a rabbit and two turtles.

Not all Swedes were shy. Some were buying many bags full of souvenirs. Why shouldn't they? It only cost them a couple of öre and everything was made with such skill and love.

The small old ladies, usually seated on neat rows of three-legged chairs behind lavishly laid tables, jumped up at the sight of 'clean-shaven tourists' and started showing off their goods. Most of the tourists bought spices and embroidered tablecloths. After a while, they discovered the beer tents by the river and headed there carrying blue-striped plastic bags full of colorful souvenirs. After a few beers in the tents, and a song or two, they climbed into their shiny Mercedes bus and left Bachkovo forever. Some of the plastic bags remained behind. Not a single old lady understood why. After all, it had taken them weeks and sometimes months to create the souvenirs. Saga took charge of distributing the left-behind goods back to their makers, carefully matching each table with its goods. She ran back and forth making loud comments about how easy it was for Swedes to forget things when they had had beer.

We had lunch at the local restaurant even though we already had two picnics. I was told off for being 'just too skinny' so I ordered a serving of French fries with grated feta cheese. Saga required lasagne and my son was happy to have a beer and meshana salata, which, by the way, is the most delicious salad in the whole wide world.

Tochka was restless. She and her husband hadn't been anywhere since the fifties when they were young communists who 'climbed mountains, read poetry to each other and sang Vysotskij songs'.

They are shooting wolves.
Who'll shoot and be a man, some cub or suckling dam?
As the beaters wave, the slavering hounds confront 'em
Blood on the snow and rows of fluttering scarlet flags.
They fixed the match, their servile lieutenants:
So superior, so sure of the route.
Bounds on liberty set with red pennants,
With their rifles held steady to shoot!
For the wolf cannot break with tradition:
When as cubs in our lair we'd entwine,
With our milk we conceived the ambition
Not ever to cross the red line…

She dried a tear as she thought of her cows. She said, "I am thinking of my cows," and started poking my father in the ribs. "Let's go NOW!" she nagged. Dad looked at her and continued sipping his beer. But the attack on his ribs escalated so he had to get up and walk down the river to fetch the car. My second cousin, aka 'T the 2d', followed him to fetch the other car and ordered Tochka to wait at the table 'like normal people'.

We didn't stop for picnics on the way back. There were cows, cats, dogs, chickens and Ivanka people waiting to be fed.

No matter how colorful its mask, I knew loneliness when I saw it. The Filmmaker was loud and opinionated, but I could tell that he was lonely. The cottage that we arrived at was his grandfather's, and it made me sad to think of times, decades and even centuries ago, when that cottage was a warm welcoming home to a loving family with real heartfelt stories to tell.

The Filmmaker had spent decades trying to spell out those same stories and failed again and again. His ability to exploit ambiguity in a way that circumvents censorship just wasn't good enough. He was anything but nostalgic about it. He was angry at the land, the cottage, the mountains and people in general. Whoever was with him that day became the target of his hatred. I became 'the embodiment of naivety and betrayal'.

After two whole days and one sleepless night of bony fingers and canes pointing at me shouting 'Get undressed, you whore!', I walked down to the nearby village and phoned Ilya.

I could almost tell that he was expecting me to call. That letter he sent me from Sweden was written in a way that allowed the assumption that he was going to be in Sofia in April hoping for a second encounter. I had just enough money for one ticket to Sofia and one back to Plovdiv so I took a bus down the mountain, said my third and final 'Goodbye' to Stoyan the puppet-maker and left for the nation's capital. I pictured Ilya perched on that same window where the kiss happened, overlooking the Mercedes logo cast in the pavement below and smiling at me in his colorful sweater while listening to *Quadrophenia*.

It wasn't at all how I'd pictured it.

He gave me clear enough directions so I was able to find his parent's flat easily. We didn't stay there long because I wanted to visit Sofia Art Academy and sign in for admission exams in the summer. Then we went to the cinema before returning to the flat for the evening.

We sat on his parents' couch talking for a while. I wanted to ease the tension so I reached for his hand and took it. We stayed holding hands for a moment, then he jumped up from the couch and opened a bottle of wine to celebrate my arrival. We drank some and waited for the rush to kick in. None came. We shared a cigarette instead. Then he played records for me.

The huge piles of vinyl featured music that almost never crossed Bulgaria's borders. First was Susan Vega, Peter Gabriel and Brian Eno. Then came Kate Bush and David Bowie. I sat quietly and listened as the music burned away every single assumption I had about good music. I had discovered an attraction that was much stronger than anything a person's physical appearance may induce.

Our bodies connected for a moment, and we stepped right into the all too familiar path of involuntary togetherness.

Mom and Dad were worried sick about me so it was a good idea to call them and tell them that I was safe, sound and 'with Ilya'. Dad mumbled something on

174

the other end, was told off by Mom and left the room cursing. She asked for details, but I wasn't going to offer any. My phone call to Plovdiv was witnessed by a dozen of Ilya's friends who came to listen to music and catch up.

26

The two remaining months of school were spent working harder than ever. I had to put my emotional life aside and concentrate on finishing school with grades good enough to apply to the academy in Sofia. Meeting Stoyan's friends in Sliven, the trip to the cottage and my short visit to Sofia had somehow reset my brain and sent it on a mission. I had no desire to be a mediocre person anymore. I didn't want to be a teacher in a godforsaken school somewhere in Bulgaria trying to teach art to children whose thoughts were occupied with drinking fathers, aging mothers, trying to figure out why communist heroes always died in the end and why that's supposed to be a good thing, screaming siblings and sometimes football and the Olympic games. Besides, even if there was a child somewhere with talent and the rare gift of insight, I wouldn't be allowed to tell her or him what I already knew about art – that it had to speak the truth, whatever its shapes and colors may be. I wanted to be an artist. I had no idea what that meant exactly in the case of a young woman like me, but I was told that I had the same chance in hell as a snowball without going to the academy. So I drew and painted as if there was a better tomorrow.

The exams were tough. I somehow knew that I did a lousy job. Spending most of the last three years dealing with Troj-shaped missing limbs, my budding sexuality, bearded fat men and God knows what, had resulted in some serious gaps in my training. I was exhausted. By the time I finished school, my belly was swollen and I was coughing like a pirate.

Mom couldn't figure out what exactly was wrong with me so she had no other choice but to take me to the doctor. She had seen very little of me since April and was convinced that I had overdone it with, among other things, 'reading, drinking, smoking and work'. The doctor examined me, took a blood test and disappeared for a while. My mother was told to step outside. When she opened the door, her face was white as a sheet. The doctor had just told her that she was going to be a grandmother.

The most remarkable thing happened that day. I was barely eighteen and although I had been a surrogate mother to Troj and Dari and knew a little about caring for children, the thought of becoming somebody's real mother should have scared me stiff. After all, being somebody's real mother meant going through every chamber of hell that my mother had gone through: sleepless nights, misery, sickness, pain, constant bickering and crying, and, above all, being forced to tolerate evil people because of…you know…family. Like Grandma Kerana, I believed in the old saying that in order to be a good person one had to 'deeply feel the burdens of the stones other people were carrying'. But some lines had to be drawn in regards to the actual stones. The only thing I could think of was that the day I became a real mother I would have the power and responsibility to make a child's life more meaningful than all our lives combined. Anybody who called my children 'disgusting', 'deviant' or 'mangals' because of their dark skin, the company they kept, or the people they loved, would suffer horrible consequences in this life and beyond. It would be my utmost pleasure to make that happen.

The wedding was supposed to be just a formality, but my family rarely missed an opportunity to celebrate. Once, we spent three days drinking because a distant relative of my mother's didn't have 'the bad kind of cancer'. He died two weeks after that. We remember him fondly.

I called an old friend who agreed to be my maid of honour and a childhood friend of Ilya's was invited to be the best man. Even T was invited. He had managed to develop a serious crush on a friend of mine so it was all decent and drama-free.

We couldn't find the right fabric for a wedding dress so we bought a cream-colored silk dress in a department store and added some stones and laces to make it less embarrassing. Mom managed to remain happy and hopeful throughout, and Dari was going crazy with excitement at the prospect of being the flower girl and the ring bearer all at once.

The ceremony was long and tedious. Two things made it particularly excruciating. One was that I felt ill and was barely managing to sit straight, let alone stand on high heels and smile. The second thing was Ilya's constant giggling. The ceremonial mistress held a long speech, accentuating the importance of our nation's safety and repeating again and again that land and duty 'goes before marriage and children'. Ilya lost his marbles more than once and giggled like the village idiot at every word she said. If I wasn't aching everywhere, I would have slapped him right there for everyone to see. My relatives wouldn't mind. A slap or two were never wrong in their eyes when a 'grown ass man giggles like a demented old woman'. His relatives couldn't possibly mind because they weren't there.

Ilya's parents came to our flat about a month or so before the wedding. They came to inspect our home and meet my parents. His mother was cold and unapologetic regarding 'these dire circumstances'. She didn't think that her son 'deserved all that extra responsibility'. After all, he was a gifted PhD student and I was the one 'who got pregnant'. I had rarely seen Mom so ashamed. She was ashamed of me, our simple flat, worn-out furniture and the sad state of our TV. "At least, the house was clean," she said after she closed the door behind them. She spent the rest of that evening sitting on the balcony smoking and looking at her plants.

They never came to the wedding. Ilya didn't seem to care much, but I could tell that my parents were really hurt. No explanations were given and no excuses were made so nobody knew why they didn't come. We didn't discuss it, but we all suspected that their visit was a test, and for some reason, we didn't pass.

Ilya stayed a couple of days after the wedding and started preparing for his departure. Mom took care of his every need. She treated him as one of her children and let him know that she cared for his well-being. She didn't ask for anything in return but 'a postcard or two maybe'. Just a day before he left for Stockholm, he told us why his parents didn't come.

Ilya had an aunt in Sofia. She was his father's older sister and as such was one of the most trusted members of his family. During the initial shock caused by my surprise pregnancy, Ilya's parents phoned her and asked her to travel to Plovdiv and 'check me out'. That she did and the information she returned with was a colorful story featuring me 'whoring around, having no less than three abortions and being the daughter of gypsies'. "Eunice," cried my mother in despair and ran out of the room.

It wasn't hard to figure out where this so-called 'information' had originated. Eunice was a midwife. Ilya's aunt was a midwife. She came, Mom and Dad were at work so she went to the only other relative living in Plovdiv and 'God bless! A colleague at that! Awww! What a lovely coincidence'. Out came the ammunition: whores, bitches, aborted demon children, illnesses and gypsies all reared their ugly heads and took Mom, Dad, Dari, me and my unborn child down.

I started bleeding almost immediately, and Dad had to drive me to the hospital in total and utter panic.

The memory of being probed and examined by many different white-coated people is vague but very much present. Somehow they managed to stop the bleeding, and I was put in a separate room to rest. I slept for two whole days.

Dad couldn't wait for Ilya to leave. He dropped him off at the train station, drove back to the house, sat me down and told me that he would do anything in his power to take care of us and protect us, no matter what happened. He was going to be my baby's father too, if need be. It was said and set in stone.

Being pregnant was like 'having one foot in the grave', I was told by family, friends and almost every other person I met, especially the elderly. Mom would order me to lay on the couch and watch TV, then feed me as if she was fattening a pig before slaughter. Dad was doing exactly the opposite. He dusted Mom's old medicine books from the '50s and read them cover to cover. The texts in these books featured communist propaganda alongside medical terms and recommendations, so he would pause and skip all the Lenin and Zivkov quotes and read the rest, devouring every line of information that was remotely relevant to the female body in general and babies and pregnancies in particular. He was the one that forced me to take walks and reduce the fat in my diet. The man was clearly on a mission, and it was driving me crazy considering the other adult in the family, Mom, just wouldn't stop shoving salami, cheese and various pickled vegetables and canned fruits down my throat.

I spent most of my days reading whatever I could find that wasn't related to medicine and longing for the immense fields where Grandpa spent his summers guarding watermelons and corn with his old beat-up rifle – the one found by Troj's feet on April 10th, 1984 – and Jana the dog. I somehow knew that if I didn't go there before my child was born, I wouldn't get another chance to lose myself in those fields, breathe in the pollen-filled air and listen to the bees. That was it. After that winter, my childhood would vanish forever together with the fields where it grew, moving like a shapeshifter from one extreme to another, making sure that life couldn't break me.

I packed a bag for myself, my sister and my six-months-pregnant belly and left for Granit.

Dari was more than happy to come with me. She told everybody on the bus that she was five years old. She wasn't. Not yet. "Are we going to Grandma and the dog?" she asked a dozen times. The answer was yes every one of those times. Apart from meeting Ivanka's beloved dog, I had promised her a visit to 'a magical place'.

Not many people know about the old oak tree in Granit. It is probably one thousand seven hundred years old. It is embedded in that same endless field where Grandpa Troj spent his summers and Troj and I went to pet donkeys. It is not the kind of field that ends abruptly as fields do in other places and other countries. This one turns into a cottage, fence, forest or an endless garden, devouring everything in its way. Small and big things flow together in the boundless greenery that swallows them in its path, etches itself deep in the rocks and weaves itself into people's short and turgid fates. It's the way fate works in those old villages.

We got off the bus and headed for 'The Tree'.

My brave little sister walked all the way there without complaining. When we reached the fence surrounding the oak tree, it was closed. We were a little late, the low metal door was locked for the summer school vacation. We had to break in, I thought and waved at Dari to follow me. But a sign next to the fence scared her and she hesitated, trampling impatiently around the fence resembling a small round thief with her striped trousers and orange t-shirt. I climbed in, lifting my pregnant belly to keep my dress from being ripped to pieces and waited for her. The old rusty sign on the fence featured a pre-Perestroika warning text and a fading picture of a very odd dog with yellow eyes and a pink piece of meat in his mouth. My sister looked at her pale arm that glowed with a kind of sunburned pink hue and refused to climb over the fence. I reached out to her, pressing my pregnant belly towards the fence and ruining my dress completely, lifted her up and promised that the dog 'had eaten his lot of pink children already a long time ago'. "In fact there was no dog," I told her. "There used to be one, but it was long dead now. They replaced him with a hundred years old woman with equally yellow eyes and the smell of well-cooked children lingering." Dari didn't appreciate my sense of humour.

Inside the fence, the green carpet of moss and ivy had fought and won a war over the feet of countless children and burdened old ladies rushing to mass. It was empty of children, grandmothers and priests. It was just resting there in the cool shade of the oak tree.

Dari was very pleased with what was promised and delivered. It was a magical place indeed. The huge tree was still growing and its branches spread out like an immense umbrella over the worn school, church and everything else inside the green fence that was also a field and a forest. Around the tree, there was a string suggesting that it took nine men to embrace the giant trunk. Nine small plastic silhouettes adorned the string as figures in a strange wedding dance. Dari felt the surface of the wire and went around a few times. She took a marker pen out of her pocket and drew hair on one of the silhouettes, 'making it female'. Then she scratched her head thinking that she should make more hairy figures in the name of fairness. I was worried about the old lady guardian of the tree so I whispered in Dari's ear. My loud whispers startled her. She dropped the cap into the ground, inserted the cap-less pen in her pocket and ran up to me.

I opened the church door and squinted. Somewhere inside the cold church awaited a chair that generations of grandmothers cared for in their own ceremonial honour. The chair had our family name on it, and I wanted to show it to my sister.

The church was empty so I threw some coins in a bowl and took a candle from the irregular mound of candles and candle stumps. Dari wrapped her arms around a big gold-plated urn by the entrance and gently caressed its surface. That was a mistake. A skinny little lady showed up from nowhere, cleared her throat, coughed and told my sister to let go of the urn. Dari's eyes filled with tears in a split second. She ran up to where I was standing but quickly stepped away. The old lady was yelling at me for chewing gum in church. I didn't understand the crime of chewing gum in church so I asked politely if it had something to do with lack of respect. "Not the case. Not the case," the woman muttered. "Chewing gum in church is like chewing them dead people's white bones," she explained. I spat out the gum quickly and wrapped it up in my chocolate-stained handkerchief. Both my sister and I disappeared behind a welcoming curtain.

Dari was noticeably bored by the time I found the chair. She had no desire to 'watch chairs' so I granted her exit, and she ran out. Outside the church, she found a bird's nest in a bush. She wanted to watch the nest for as long as it took to learn everything about it. Little sisters cared more for a bird's nest than boring church chairs, I was told. We dug up small pieces of paper from the bottom of my bag, wrote our names on them and hung them around the deserted nest for generations to come.

Behind the school, we found a peach tree. It was the first Dari had ever seen. A drawing was produced, a kind of a peach certificate was issued and a small peach was crafted out of the play dough she found in her other, ink-free pocket. We both simultaneously wondered if picking some peaches for Ivanka was a good idea. The skinny old lady read our minds and pointed to the rusty sign reminding us of our long outstayed welcome.

The sunset was blooming with orange flames by the time we climbed back into the street and out of the mossy green kingdom. Living in the village meant long summer evenings that start with lunch, somehow lead to dinner and end with liqueur and songs. Dari sat quietly most of the evening. Her mouth was frozen half-open and she sat perfectly still listening to the Bearded Lady sing. Dad's aunt was visiting another relative but couldn't resist seeing my pregnant belly so she stopped by for supper. That particular evening, she sang 'this old bag of bones' favourite', featuring gypsy virgins burning with desire, embracing muscular black (for some mysterious reason unknown to anyone but her) bodies and filling them with fire from their bulging loins.

Outside the house, the green field had finally embraced and swallowed the sun. I watched my little sister fall asleep in my arms, and my grandmother fussed about the table, pouring tea and removing leftovers for the dog. I felt the life growing in me thinking that one day I will do that same journey with my child and run around the oak tree, look for church chairs and steal peaches.

Decades later, I went back with my youngest child Saga. Ivanka was long gone and so were the pumpkin fields and the animals. But the church and the school were still there serving a different kind of community that was a lot more Romani than before. The village had finally surrendered to those who were willing to stay there and take care of the land.

The field had shrunk, its growth hampered by new buildings and new wild and overgrown gardens, fairly reminiscent of Grandma Kerana's.

We stayed just long enough for our mother to start panicking. I knew that sooner rather than later, Dad would arrive in his old light-blue car, pack a bag of groceries and leave with Dari and me dragging our feet behind with even more groceries and a headless dead chicken courtesy of Ivanka. Mom greeted us with hugs and enough food to feed a small army. I excused myself and headed to the bedroom to rest.

Doctor appointments became a regular thing after the incident with Ilya's aunt. I took the bus to the clinic every week during my eighth month of pregnancy, and Dad drove me during the ninth month. My due date was December 24th and just about every child and adult in our building mentioned Christmas every time they saw me waddling around in my heavy coat leaning on Dad's old umbrella.

It was a snowy December and the roads and sidewalks were covered with ice. Mom explicitly forbade me to go anywhere. I was only permitted to go to the clinic, which I did every week until December 20th when inspired by some children ice-skating, I made a little dance step slipped, and fell to the ground crashing through the surface of a frozen paddle. My water broke.

Dad was waiting for me in the parking lot. He saw me fall and ran to pick me up. Upon seeing the yellowish fluid running down my legs, he grabbed me and more or less carried me to the clinic. I was picked up in an ambulance and driven to the nearest hospital, which happened to be in the Romani neighbourhood.

Something very strange was making itself present. I was told that women experienced excruciating pain when they gave birth, but this was something else. It was a powerful force of nature trying to break through my body, no matter what damage it caused. It started slowly and then hit me harder and harder from the inside, forcing itself out. I obeyed it as much as I could. I didn't make a sound other than ask for water and a bigger pillow. Hearing other women scream was disturbing enough. I was laid down on one of the seven beds in a large hall lit with fluorescent lights so bright that they hurt my eyes. I felt disoriented. The noise was almost unbearable, and the nurse assigned to me had a nasty cough.

There was only one doctor there that night. She was young but extremely efficient. She ran her troops like a general and everyone seemed to come out of their screaming infernos with their limbs and sanities intact. Finally, she came to me, waved the midwife away, adjusted my pillow and told me that she too had children. "Trust me," she whispered a second before she ordered the nurse to climb on me and jump on my belly. Soon after that, a lightning hit my brain, somebody cried in the distance and I blacked out.

Hours later, I woke up wondering where I was. It was morning and the sun was shining on the bare yellow walls of an unfamiliar room. I raised my head to look around, but the sudden movement caused a sharp pain below my waist. I cried out. Seconds later, my mother's voice echoed in the corridor, and she slammed the door open carrying a small baby boy.

"I found him. I found him in the room where you gave birth. He was so peaceful and happy that they forgot him there. Assholes! I hate this place so much!"

She lifted his tiny body and placed him carefully on my chest. She was crying.

"Why are you crying, Mama? Aren't you happy? Isn't he beautiful?"

"He is. But...but...I'm sorry! He looks just like..."

"No, Mom, please, don't! He is TOTALLY new. Do you hear me? NEW!"

"I know but...he looks just like Him."

"Mom, I warn you...I will never speak to you again if you keep this up. He is his own person. Do you want him to grow up thinking he came to replace somebody else? Do you?"

She turned around and started walking towards the door. The small child on my chest was smiling. His eyes were deep and wide-open, and although he couldn't yet focus, he was staring right at me.

Third Regional was even older than the City Hospital where Mom worked. Everything was old, from the worn-out wooden furniture that had been painted at least a dozen times, to the half-deaf nurses that spent more time chain-smoking than doing their jobs. The hospital staff called this wing 'The Cunt Factory' – an ugly name for a place where mostly Romani babies were born. The nurses hated the mothers and the mothers hated the nurses.

Mom had no authority there because it wasn't her hospital, but she would put her white coat on and sneak in as often as she could until every single nurse knew what she was up to. They didn't like it one bit. 'The Cunt Factory' had very little tolerance for outsiders, especially 'privileged' City Hospital people. Mom tried to get us out of there sooner than the obligatory one week behind closed doors but couldn't.

I was sharing a room with a kind Romani woman who had just given birth to her fifth baby. Every day, an old, often sickly nurse would come into the room, take the babies and wash them under running water in the sink. I loathed these medieval morning rituals and thought that nothing could be worse than seeing one's baby boy being washed by an old sickly woman over a broken sink. But it got worse. After running into Mom lurking around in her City Hospital coat, the nurse got even rougher with the babies. She came into the room one morning, grabbed my son by his feet like a chicken about to become dinner, carried him to the sink and started washing him with soap. He cried out, but she filled his mouth with soap and water. I tried to stop her, but she was stronger than an ox so I bit her and tore the baby out of her arms. It took hours to calm my son down. The bite marks on the old nurse's arm earned me the well-deserved nickname 'Teen Bitch'.

I didn't sleep for three days after the sink incident. I threw so many fits that the nurses gave up and let me have my son in a basket next to my bed. Being ignored was fine with me, but they started harassing my Romani roommate. They would scream at her for not giving her baby water. I thought that not giving babies water was a good thing. She breastfed her baby all the time so there was no need for water, formula or anything else. But it didn't matter, all those years living in Tracia taught me that Romani people were treated badly no matter what they did.

Poor Marja. She had no reason to be kind to me or anyone like me, but she was. Besides, she was funny and full of mischief, which made my stay at Third Regional almost bearable. And she had an enormous family. There were about a hundred of them, and they all looked like they could be siblings. The whole lot of them would come to the hospital followed by a full-on orchestra carrying beat up violins, accordions and a giant drum and serenade us until the nurses marched out to chase them away.

The short skinny man in the oversized double-breasted suit, who I assumed was her husband, would lead the family to the hospital wall and shout, "Show me my son!" But every time my roommate showed him the baby, the now chubby well-fed child would start crying and turn blue, which caused a lot of discontent amongst the members of his large family. Rude jokes about the 'likeness in complexion' were uttered loudly and with audible vigour. They tossed the father back and forth and laughed demanding to see the baby again. This went on for a week.

No men were allowed to enter the premises. Dad didn't want to cause any problems for me so every afternoon after work he would patiently wait underneath our window waving and smiling as soon as I appeared in the narrow window frame. Our room was on the third floor so he probably saw very little of his grandchild despite my incredibly imaginative window displays. He just smiled and waved.

On the day of our release, Mom managed to bribe one of the night nurses to bring me a set of clean clothes. My light-blue trousers and a new lace top were neatly packed in a plastic Marlboro bag – a sign of prosperity – together with a small baby onesie and a freshly knitted jacket and a tiny hat. I don't know where my mother found the mohair yarn, but these baby clothes were spectacular. She must have used all of her December lunch coupons for that.

I was more than happy to leave the maternity ward of Third Regional. My face was already hurting from smiling wider than my muscles would allow. Dad looked happy and a little scared. His favourite light-blue shirt was buttoned all the way up to his chin, and I could barely see his face for the immense flower bouquet in his arms. Next to him, hugging his left leg, stood my little sister, dressed in a blue flowery dress wearing a hair bow bigger than her face. Typical of my mother to color-match us all, I thought and stood for a couple of seconds admiring them. Dad handed the giant bouquet over to Dari, thus creating a mountain of flowers with a little girl underneath gasping for air and walked over to me with his arms stretched. I surrendered the baby without as much as a sound. He leaned over, touched his tiny happy face and whispered: "I know Iva disapproves but just this once…Hello, Troj! You can leave now."

My son's face relaxed, his eyes closed slowly and he fell asleep in Dad's arms only slightly trembling when a tear or two landed on his cheek.

*